Shattered by Shame, Restored by Grace

©Copyright 2015 Megan Sullivan

Published by August Grace Publishing LLC

126 LeFleurs Drive

Vicksburg, MS 39180

www.meganlafaith.com

ISBN 978-0-692-54427-3

The book recaptures the events of Megan Sullivan according to the author's recollection and perspective. While the stories are true,some names and identifying details have been changed to protect the privacy of those involved.

Dedication

Through my pain, I found my purpose,

And through my pain God didn't allow me to become drained,

He knew I needed perseverance in the rain,

For as I looked above to hear His voice and to see His glory shine so bright,

I knew that God had given me enough tenacity to fight this fight

As shame shattered in my face, I knew that God had given me sufficient Grace

To My Daughter – Madison Grace

I dedicate this book to those who helped me keep faith in God during this trying time. Because of you, I'm able to revive my story to share and uplift others.

–Laurence and Leah Sullivan, Bishop Oscar and Loretta Davis, and Valerie O'Quinn–

Table of Contents

Introduction

Now let me start off by saying in no way shape or form would I have imagined myself writing a book, yes throughout school I was a pretty good writer but it was nothing that I thought I would do to inspire others. I felt as though God was tugging in my spirit to write this book and share my message with others, to show that negative situations have a positive impact on your life. I was very nervous about exposing this portion of my life because this was very sacred to me and I was ashamed of the events that were occurring in my life. I never thought about exposing my secrets to help someone else make it through the same storm I encountered. Every storm ends with a beautiful rainbow.

As I began writing this book, I wanted to share my story raw, hiding no details but allowing people to see that there not the only one that go through trials and tribulations, and they don't have to ashamed of their story. In life, we all feel a sense of rejection but rejection isn't always negative, but it refines your imperfections and restore your joy. I intended for this book to play as if you and I were having a casual conversation over the phone and you were asking me how did I make through and what advice would I give you. By any chance, am I any better than anyone but a friend whom is trying to uplift you through the trying times.

While writing my book there were many days, I sat to myself and asked was a qualified enough to write this book, were people going to be accepting on my book, but God told me to continue because I was going to be a blessing unto others, and he was using me as a blessing to bless others so he could bless me. He spoke to me and told me what you went through wasn't just for you but it was for you to bless those who are encountering the same journey as you did, and you can uplift them, and tell them to cast their cares on me, the Lord of the Upmost High God.

I went through many titles when writing this book, but the title *Shattered by Shame, Restored by Grace* captured my attention because being a young lady, unmarried, and pregnant brings about a lot of pain, shame, and sadness, but by God's grace we are able to overcome the negativity and be bold in the Word of God. The thing about God is that when we think we have made a mistake He already knows what we are going to do before we do it. Therefore, He makes provision for us rather than division from us. His grace and mercy is fresh every day, and His faithfulness remains steadfast.

I want this to be a place where you can be yourself and free yourself from the outside world, and you allow your trials to make you better rather than make you bitter. For we can do all things through Christ who strengthens us, and we are mighty and strong in his Word.

Now follow me in my journey as how one true mother's pain adds love and fulfillment to her destiny.

The Beginning of a New Ending

In the summer of 2010, Facebook was the empire of social media, from finding out the latest gossip, internet thugs, relationships beginning, and meeting new people. If you weren't on Facebook, you were basically a lame. I mean everybody wanted to post pics of everything they did, and this was a way for people to communicate who were afraid to talk to you in person.

Throughout the years, I would have people to approach me in my inbox trying to date and talk to me but I wouldn't give them the time of the day because I felt like that was such an inappropriate way to come to me, especially if you see me every day and you can't open your mouth to even say hello, I mean like really, that is such a weak minded move.

All through my college years, I would have a boyfriend back at home, but at the same time I would have my friend guys at school I would mess around with, which was typical for everybody in college, but hey it was all fun in games. Nobody was really serious, all people cared about honestly was sex, partying, and having fun. Now don't get me wrong I was partying, having fun and going to class, but I wasn't participating in the sexual activities.

During the summer of 2010, I decided to stay at home and commute back and forth to summer school, because I didn't want to take a lot of hours during the fall, so I decided to take a Health and Economics course. I lived about forty miles, from the college I attended, as I was driving down the highway, I would like Facebook statuses, *I know that wasn't safe at all*, but hey I was a typical young person, and I thought I was invincible.

During the summer, I was talking to a guy back home, and he and I favorite song was "Already Taken" by Trey Songz, so I wrote a status and it stated

"I don't want to be a player, Baby I'm taken, I just want to love my baby, I'm already taken".

Trey knew it was aimed at him, so he put lol under the status, and I replied back hilariously "Glad you find it entertaining". I pulled in the parking lot at school, and I had about twenty minutes before class started, so I sat in the car and I went straight to Facebook, I mean I was Facebook addict, and I had a notification stating someone commented on my status, so I chuckled because I knew that was probably my best friend being messy, because she knew that was my guy friend and I song we had for one another. As I checked the status it was a guy name Mark, and WHOM EVER HAS YOU TAKEN IS A LUCKY GUY, looking strangely and confused at the Facebook comment, I was trying to gather if I knew or remembered this guy from anywhere. Hurriedly, I clicked to take a look at his profile, looking through all his friends, pictures, and wall posts.

Suddenly it clicked in my head that this was my homegirl Jay boyfriend cousin. Only seeing him maybe once or twice, I vaguely had him in mind. After sitting and pondering trying to remember the last time I had seen him, it dawned on me that I had met him the previous year in the mall, but I really did pay him any mind because I was trying to shop, and he really wasn't my type. Eventually, I commented back and told him, YEP THE GUY WHO HAS ME TAKEN IS LUCKY BECAUSE I'M ONE OF A KIND.

From there we responded back and forth, as eventually he began making flirtatious remarks, and at that moment, I decided to stop replying to the post, because I didn't want him to get the wrong perception. I went to class, and all through class my phone continuously buzzed consistently, and when my professor wasn't looking I would take a look at my phone, but it wasn't a text message or missed call so it could only be a notification from Facebook.

As I left class, Trey called me,

Excitedly I answered the phone, "Hey bae! What you doing",

His response very dry and bitter, so

"What is wrong with you", and there was long silent pause…

"Hello, Hello, Hello" *glancing at the phone to make sure the call didn't disconnect,*

"What's going on under your Facebook status,"

Instantly, I knew what he was referring too, and the back of my mind I was like this was the crap that I was trying to avoid from the start.

With a sly deep breath of grief "It was nothing, and that was one of Jay's friend, and I really didn't even know the guy so you don't have anything to worry about"

But of course, he thought I was lying, so to avoid confrontation about the insignificant matter, I just hung up the phone and gave him time to get over his foolish and insecure ways.

Christy called and asked me to meet her at her dorm, so I rode over there to hang out. We were up the room laughing and cracking jokes on people, I was telling her about the Mark commenting under my status on Facebook status, and how Trey was tripping on the comments because he assumed I was messing around with Mark.

As we were talking, I checked my Facebook and Mark had written me in my inbox on Facebook, and I showed Christy, and "Girllll you know how I feel about dudes in my inbox that is a no go for m." Laughing hysterically, she replied saying "Sweetie, and I know when you right, a good way to get that tail put to the left right quick" we fell all over ourselves cracking up.

Now normally, I wouldn't even respond to the message, but for some odd reason I decided to respond and give Mark some conversation. So as we writing each other through our Facebook inboxes the conversations began getting deeper and more interesting. I will give it to Mark, his conversations kept me on my feet, and I began feeling myself getting intrigued by conversation, but I vowed to not let myself get in deep because I wasn't trying to get in a relationship with this guy nor catch feelings.

As the days went by, we would write each other from the break of day to the dawn of night, from talking about life's issues, goals and dreams, friendships, and just cracking jokes and laughter. If anyone knows me, if you can me laugh you can become my best friend.

One day he decided to ask me for my phone number, and I had made up in my mind previously that I wasn't going to give in to him easily. So I told him I DON'T KNOW YOU WELL ENOUGH TO GIVE YOU MY PHONE NUMBER Thinking back on something's, previously I thought that he had attempted to get with Christy's homegirl, and I didn't dare want to get myself involved in any drama. As he and I conversed through Facebook, I stated: THAT I DIDN'T THINK THAT WOULD BE THE BEST IDEA, SAYING THAT I HAD HEARD AT ONE POINT HE WAS INVOLVED WITH A FEMALE, AND AT THE SAME TIME HE HAD A CHILD WHICH ADDED BABY MAMA DRAMA.

During this time I was way too young, and I was ready to experience the role of dealing with a crazy baby mama and playing step mama. Yep, I was pretty judgmental because if you had a child I didn't want to even affiliate myself with you. He responded reluctantly, DESCRIBING HE WAS SINGLE, AND HE WASN'T IN A RELATIONSHIP WITH ANYONE, AND HE PROMISED THAT HE DIDN'T HAVE ANY BABY MAMA DRAMA BECAUSE HIS BABY MAMA KNEW HER PLACE AND THAT THEY ARE ONLY IN CONVERSATION FOR THE SAKE OF HIS DAUGHTER'S NEEDS. That little petty speech spill still didn't persuade me at all to give him my number, so I told him NO.

After me telling him no, he still consistently wrote me on Facebook, and over conversations carried on as normal, but he began asking a lot of questions about me and he seemed to genuinely be interested in me not only by looks but my personality. Of course, I began catching feelings because of the in-depth conversations he and I were having. One day as we writing, and he and I were having a deep, intense conversation about relationships and how we both felt as though God should be center point for a successful relationship. That was the most attractive thing he could have ever done, and I told him to text me and gave him my number. He made a smart remark saying I knew you would give in, who could resist him, and I laughed and told him don't get cocky and arrogant because he could easily get left behind. I might have been laughing, but I was very serious about the statement I made.

Immediately after giving him my number, my phone started ringing, and as when I looked at the phone it was an unfamiliar number so I knew it had to be him. Sweat began dripping from my forehead, my palms were getting, and my head was spinning a thousand miles an hour, I was so nervous because I was expecting him to call this soon, and I didn't know what to say over the phone because I didn't want to mess up the great moments we had, so right before the call went to voicemail I answered the phone in a sweet, innocent, but sexy voice

"Hey, who is this calling Megan",

"This is Mark", *with that elementary chuckle when you find out a little boy likes you on the playground,*

From there the conversation started as if we knew each other all our life. The days would turn into nights, and the nights would turn into days; that is how long we communicate with each other, and if we weren't on the phone, we were texting. There was never a silent moment on the phone with the two of us because the conversations were so intriguing.

Mark and I had been talking for about two weeks now, and he told me that he was coming down to visit some of his family because they were having a cook-out in Vicksburg and that he would like to see me. Butterflies rose in my stomach, but yet I was jumping up and down like a little kid in a candy store because I was ecstatic of seeing him. You know your girl couldn't show him that she was that excited. I told him that would be cool, but it would have to be later that evening because I had some things to do earlier that day, but I had already planned in my mind, how I would make this day for him memorable and remarkable. As soon as I got off the phone with him, I called my best friend, and told her that Mark was coming down to Vicksburg, and we need to go shop so I can find the perfect out and accessories to sweep him off his feet. My bestie was like cool, we can go by the outlet mall first thing tomorrow, and I was like cool that's a bet!

Before we hung up the phone, I told her girl wait a minute, I'm all excited about Mark coming down, but I still have been conversing with Trey, and even though he and I weren't in a relationship I felt as though some boundaries shouldn't be crossed. I began feeling bad about meeting Mark in my hometown when I knew there was a chance of Trey seeing us together, but I had gotten myself in so deep with Mark, I felt as though there was no turning back. As I was lying the bed thinking, I told myself I was intuned into making others happy and satisfied till the point, and I risk hurting others feelings whereas I'm limiting my own happiness.

The next day, my best friend called and told me that she wasn't going to be able to come to the outlet mall with me because she had to run some errands with her mom. I went to the outlet mall, to the store "Rue 21", I was looking for something appealing and sexy but nothing too revealing, but also something that had the colors related to the 4th of July. As I was searching through the clothes racks, I felt like I could find nothing that I envisioned in my mind, everything was either too short, too tight, too loose or just not cute at all. I left the outlet mall, and went to Dillards, and I found the perfect blue and white spaghetti strap shirt, with small accent flowers, and the shirt buttoned down the back, and some cute white, not hoochie mama, shorts. As I tried the clothes on, I was like this right here is going to be the banging outfit.

On the fourth of July, I was at home hanging out with family and friends cracking jokes, reminiscing on old times, eating BBQ, and just having a good time. The night of the 4th everybody head downtown to the big firework show on the river. Well, this particular I had plans to go with someone else rather than my family. Mark called me earlier that day and told me he had made it town, and that he was at his family house in my hometown at the cookout, so I told him before I head out to the firework show I would come pick him up so we could go together. I was extremely nervous because this was the first time we were meeting up in person.

During this time I had a white Dodge Avenger, I made sure the car was spotless inside and outside because I wanted to make a lasting first impression. As I drove to pick him up, my heart was pounding, but I couldn't allow myself to get too worked up because I had to make sure my makeup didn't mess up from the excessive sweat of nervousness. Mark walked to the car looking real good, in my mind I was like *"Damn, I got to make sure I keep him on my team",* so he got in the car said hey and kind of gave me that sexy wink and told me I looked nice. I giggled and said thank you, and you look pretty nice yourself.

We made it to the firework show, and there were tons of people there, and I just made up in my mind that if ran into Trey, it is what it is, at the end of the day I was single. As we walked pass and through the crowd of people to get a clear view of the fireworks, we went up on hill in a hotel parking lot, were the view was perfect. As the fireworks lit up the sky, bursting with beautiful rays, and loud popping noise, Mark moved behind me and held me at my waist as the fireworks were bursting. My body started feeling all jitterly and lovey dovey, and I enjoyed the moment.

Mark whispered in my ear while grabbing my by waist, "Are you enjoying the view"

Tickinglsy "Of course"

What he didn't know was that I was enjoying him more than anything. At that very moment, I just knew that this guy was God sent, and this was the birth of a true love story. The fireworks show had ended, traffic was packed on every road possible, so we had a serious wait time, as we were in traffic we begin talking and laughing, and suddenly we both reached in to kiss one another. The kiss wasn't just any type of peck, but it was long intimate exhilarating kiss. So after our lips parted off one another, he looked at me and smiled, and said girl you know you fast kissing on me, and laughed and said boy please you know you were the one that kissed me. We made it back to his Uncle to drop him off, and he got out the car and said I had a great time with you today, and this won't be our last time. I was blushing so hard, I believe my dark skin started turning red, and my eyes got so slant I could barely see.

After spending time with one another on the 4th of July, something both sparked in us about one another, and we knew we wanted to take the next step in our relationship. After about two weeks after the first visit, we decided to turn our friendship into an official relationship. I don't jump into relationships quickly, but when I do I obviously feel very passionate about that person, so I told him I would like for him to meet my parents. He meets my parents, and he and my mom seemed to really click and get alone, and I was surprised at my dad because I thought he would be stern, mean, and threaten to kill the boy, but he was really nice and just asked Mark about himself and his goals in life.

Now let me mention, I didn't tell my parents that he had a child, because I wasn't sure how they would look upon that. I kind of felt as though my parents would prefer me not to date anyone with a child, but we never discussed that issue either. So I just thought that I should hold off on telling them that piece information until they really got to know Mark.

After he met my parents, he invited me to meet his parents, his dad and I hit off perfectly, we were laughing and he was cracking jokes on me, I mean it felt like I had known his dad forever. Now his mom, on the other hand, was a little stand offish, which was honestly fine by me because I wasn't in this relationship to date his family, but just him, that was just the type of mind set I had. She kept asking me how old I was, and what did I do, so I told her at that time I was twenty years old, which was four years younger that son, and she felt as though I was too young, and she really didn't want to know how I felt about her. I told her I was an honors student at Alcorn, and I majored in Geographic Information Sciences and Homeland Security Science, and from there she knew I wasn't just any kind of flunky wanting her son because I had my own before he came in the picture. Over time she began to warm up to me till the point she would call me more than she called her own son.

Mark told me that he never brought any girl around his daughter because he respected her enough to only bring her around those whom we knew he would keep in his life for the long run, and I totally respected that. After about two weeks of us in an official relationship, he decided it was time for us his daughter, Myra and I to meet one another, and I was really shocked. It made me feel that this guy entrusts me and expects that we are in it for the long haul to bring his daughter around. He warned that his daughter didn't really warm up to people, and he was basically trying to say that she would probably shun away from me, and even his dad stated I would be surprised if Myra let you get close to her daddy. In a way, I was somewhat nervous to meet her, but at the same time I knew I had a special touch for children.

Mark invited me to his family reunion, and this was the day I was going to have the privilege of meeting his daughter. When I pulled up at his mom house, he and his daughter came out the house to greet me at my car. He introduced us to one another, and she smiled and leaned her head on her dad's shoulder. As they were walking in front of me into the house, I had an epiphany and I wanted one day when I had my daughter to have a bond with her father as those two had established. When we got the house, his daughter ran to me and she took to me very well. It was so crazy, she was so attached till the point she didn't want her dad nor anybody who asked to get her. Mark was extremely surprised, and he asked me what I did to his daughter in a jokingly manner because she never reacted like this to a new person. I told him children know when people are genuinely nice and caring, and that was the aroma I had about myself.

As I relationship began to grow and our love became deeper with one another, I treated his daughter as is she was my very own child, from buying her clothes, toys, feeding her, and letting her spend the night at home without her dad. He and I would take her on summer trips to places like SeaWorld, the aquarium, and zoo. It got to the point where my family considered her a part of us, and my parents loved her as if she was their grandchild. We established a bond as a true family. I will never forget the day, he and I were having an argument, and we didn't think she noticed, and she hollered at both of us telling us to stop because we were supposed to be family and love on one another. From that point, I truly knew that there was an unbreakable bond that she, her father, and I had established, and we couldn't allow disagreements to keep us off focus.

After about a couple of months into our relationship, we began to have sexual encounters, because I truly loved and trust him. I knew that God had sent this man just for me, and I felt secure that I could give him a piece of me that I hadn't offered others I found interest in. The encounters were happening only occasions till the point every time we spent time together, we had the urge to have sex.

Now I knew that it was unholy and sin, but I would ask God to forgive me every time I bowed down to flesh. I decided to get on birth control because I didn't want to run the risk of having a child that I knew I wasn't prepared for, and then at the same time he had already had a child out of wedlock, and adding a child to my life before marriage was something that I declared wouldn't happen to me because I had an image to uphold.

One day he and I were in such an urge and heated situation to have sex, and Mark told me that he didn't have a condom. So immediately told him well we will just have to wait because I didn't want to run that risk.

"Baby I promise I will pull out, and furthermore you're on birth control so you have nothing to worry about".

As I sat in the bed with my arms folded, " NO!"

He began to rubbing on my body in all the right places, and BAM!! You know the rest is all she wrote.

Throughout the years we go on couple vacations to pro-football and basketball games, we would have weekly date nights, I would spend the night at his apartment at least 2 times out of the week or if not we wouldn't miss a weekend together. At one point, it felt like when you saw him you would see me, and if you saw me, you would see him. That's just how much we enjoyed each other's company. Even though at times we would have disagreements, the love and laughter we shared outweighed the bad.

Now while, yes things were going good, at times I had my doubts Mark was being unfaithful, but I never let those thoughts play long and hard in my head. At the beginning of our relationship, I didn't take things too seriously so I was still doing my thing messing around and chilling with guys from my past relationship and friendships, but once I saw the serious and the potential greatness he and I had together, I became fully committed to him and only him. You couldn't pay me to even give anybody any attention.

We Got Some Moves To Make

I graduated from college in May of 2012 with my B.S. degree in Geographic Information Systems. My ultimate goal was to land a governmental job in my hometown as GIS Analyst or to become a Geospatial Engineer at the NASA branch on the coast of Mississippi. I had two interviews in MS, but I didn't get either job, so at this point I had no choice but to apply for jobs out of state, and I didn't want to do that because that would put a strain on my relationship with my boyfriend. And I knew that he was settled with his job and it would be hard for him to move because he didn't want to leave his daughter behind.

I received a job interview with a very prestigious direct mail marketing company in Birmingham AL as a GIS Technician, and the interview went great! Yes, I was excited about the potential job, but at the same time was it worth me risking my relationship.

Mark and I really took this situation pretty hard because true enough during the summer time I attended numerous internships where I had to go out of town for one to three months but if I received a job out of town that would be totally different because that would be permanent. So I received the callback from the interview and they told me the job was mine, and I was jumping and dancing all inside but I had to remain calm on the phone. After getting the call, I hurriedly called my mom and dad and told them I got the job! They were excited about the new journey I was embarking upon.

Suddenly it dawned on me that I had to tell Mark. I knew he would be excited that I got the job but not that it was out of state. I finally built up the courage to call him. As he answered the phone,

I paused for about twenty seconds, "Hey bae."

"What's wrong with your phone?"

"Nothing. I have some exciting, but bad news at the same time."

"Tell me. Don't hold back."

"The people from the job in Alabama gave me a call and told me that I was a perfect fit, and they would like for me to start within two weeks."

Mark paused for a second and said joyfully in a low tone, "I'm happy for you, baby. You deserve it."

I asked, "Are you really happy for me, or are you just saying that because that's the right thing to say?"

"I'm happy for you because you have a job that's offering you all the things you desire for your career."

At that moment, I really started feeling excited about my career path. I asked him, "Now how are we going to make our relationship work, with you in Mississippi and me in Alabama?"

He said, "Honestly, I don't know."

I paused for a very long time because I didn't know whether to catch an attitude and become pissed off or to try to see where he was coming from. So I asked him, "What the does that mean?"

"I mean I don't know because that's a great bit of distance between us. And it's not like you are up there for a couple of months; you're actually going to be living there for good."

"Would you consider moving, since your job is transferable?"

Mark sighed. "It isn't that easy to just get up and leave."

"Why not?"

"I have a daughter, and I can't leave her behind. And you know I want to be there for her financially."

I thought, *Money travels, and he could easily get her on the weekends, seeing it's only three hours away.* But, of course, I realized I was being selfish.

I told him at this point I had no other job opportunity awaiting, and that this job offer was just too exceptional to turn down, and he said he understood.

I began tearing up on the phone, with my relationship failing right before my eyes. I had to choose between my career and my relationship, which I had literally put years into. I was willing to fight till the end of time to keep my relationship because I loved Mark with all my heart; he was truly my first love.

As I was crying, he began crying over the phone, saying, he didn't want to me leave but he also wanted to see me succeed in life, and he knew that I deserved the best.

"Don't worry, baby," he said. "We're going to work through this, and we'll come up with a plan to make this work."

"I don't want to lose you, baby."

As the days went on, I began receiving emails from my new job about turning in paperwork and allocating me relocation expenses, so at this point everything was turning from a dream to reality. I began packing my clothes, electronics, buying new furniture, and hunting for an apartment; it was all such a bittersweet moment.

I began shedding tears in my room. I knew I was making a lifetime choice. I was toggling in my mind if it was worth the risk, weighing the pros and cons, but the Lord whispered to me that all things work together for the good of those that are pleasing unto to sight.

I stood on the Word of God and believed that He would give Mark and me the strength for the survival of our relationship.

Before I left, my parents and friends gave me a farewell barbecue on my landing a new job and venture in life. We all laughed and joked around, but Mark was a little stand-offish for a while, which I just shook off.

After everyone left that night, I asked him, "What's wrong?"

He lowered his head and said, "Nothing."

At that point I knew it was something, so I asked again, "What's really going on?"

"I have a lot on my mind—you wouldn't understand."

Furious, I blurted out, "You are being very selfish at this point because everybody else is happy about my success, but yet and still you are up here with a chip on your shoulder, like somebody has done something to you, when clearly I haven't done anything." I just stood and stared at him.

He said remorsefully, "You right. Go live your life then, and make all the money in the world. I ain't stopping you at all."

"I know you're not, but you're being selfish, and this isn't helping the relationship at all."

Mark grabbed his keys. "We will talk about this later," he said. "You have an attitude, and I don't have time to deal with all of this."

"Okay. Fine."

After he left, I called him about an hour later to make sure he'd made it home safely, and his response was, "I didn't think you cared enough to check on me."

"Just because you make me mad doesn't mean I just stop caring."

That was a typical Mark response. Whenever he was in the wrong, he always tried reverse psychology, as if everything was my fault, but I wasn't going for that crap that particular day.

The night before I left, I stayed with him, and we cuddled and shared our emotions with one another. We both decided that after I got settled in at my new job and the new city, that he would begin seeing how he could either transfer his job to Alabama or if he could become certified in Alabama as a tech and get a job within the hospital.

After hearing that, I felt a weight fall off my shoulders because I knew that he would give his all in making this relationship work, and he wanted the relationship just as bad as I did.

After moving to Alabama, things were going great, from landing the perfect job in corporate America working from eight to five, with great pay and benefit incentives. Hey, I was living the best life for a college graduate. Not only was my career going great, I felt like I was growing more in Christ, and my relationship with Mark was on level ten.

Every other weekend I would drive to Mississippi to see my family and boyfriend. Or if I didn't go home, they would come to visit me. Mark would come down and bring his daughter, and I would be so excited to see her. I would have a gift for every time because I loved her like she was my child.

Mark would plan romantic date nights for us when I came home, and it would just light me up inside. I knew he was the man for me.

Suddenly he began slacking on coming to Alabama, and he would give me random excuses like, he had worked all week, he was tired and didn't feel like driving. Or he would tell me that driving back and forth was making him spend a lot of his money, and that was hurting his budget because he had bills to pay at his own apartment.

And true enough at first, I was blindsided and I accepted the excuses. I told him, "Well, that's fine since I come home at least two to three times out of the month."

Then we began arguing over little things, such as if I called him and he didn't answer. Which was odd, because I'd never had this problem with him.

He began hanging out with his boys all the time and would stay out late all night. Now don't get me wrong. I didn't mind him at all going out and having a good time with his homeboys, but it came down to a recurring thing. I knew the type of guys he hung out with wasn't always up to doing the right thing, being single or in a relationship. They had chicks on the brain.

He would tell me that he didn't trip when I hung out with friends and that I needed to stop tripping because it made him feel as though I didn't trust him. Like I explained to him, "For one, you wouldn't trip with me hanging out with my friends for the simple fact that you know the girls I hang out with ain't on no childish, immature crap. And then, furthermore, I don't get back home three and four o'clock in the morning, so I have yet to give you a valid reason to act a fool."

He was steadily running down to New Orleans with his homeboys but was complaining about money when it came down to visiting me, his own girlfriend. That wasn't logically adding up in my mind.

I got to the point where, in my mind, *I should just cut him off.* It was too many men in my area for me to be dealing with him when he wasn't putting in any effort. Friends from Alabama and I would go downtown to the bar or go out to happy hour, and guys would holla at me and ask me on dates, but my loving heart wouldn't allow me to give these men the time of day. Now these weren't average men; they were doctors, lawyers, and financial consultants. But I was so in love, all I wanted was Mark. Even though he knew how to piss me off the very ends of this earth, I felt as though he was irreplaceable.

I slacked off questioning him about going out with his boys since he said I didn't trust him. Of course, I wanted the relationship to work, so I decided to just keep giving it a try.

One weekend I came home to visit Mark. As I pulled up, he came and grabbed my bags out the car we walked up the stairs and he told me to wait in the living room. I kept asking him why I couldn't go past the living room, and he said, "Don't worry about it. Just do what I say."

When he came back to the front, he and he had surprised and cooked me a nice romantic dinner, and he even had me a daiquiri, *even though it was store bought it was the thought that mattered.* As he and I were eating, reminiscing, and laughing, he told me to hurry and finish eating because he was taking me out to the movies. I was very surprised saying that lately all we were doing were arguing and fussing with one another, so to give me all this attention was shocking.

When Mark came and got my bags out of the car when I made it, he'd left his cell phone on the armrest of the couch where I was sitting. Now the whole time we were eating it never dawned on me to even look at his phone even though I knew it was sitting there, but all of a sudden it keep vibrating and I could see the messages come through the on the banner of the screen.

One message came through and it was an unsaved number, but the message said; YEAH, I AND MY BOYFRIEND ARE HAVING ISSUES SO I DECIDED TO LET HIM GO.

At that point, I thought, *What the hell is really going on?*

Mark was in the kitchen washing dishes. I didn't say anything right away. I was waiting for another message to come through, not wanting to overreact. So the next message came through asking, SO WHAT ARE YOU GOING TO DO ABOUT YOUR GIRLFRIEND?

After seeing that, I walked in the kitchen all quietly and calmly. He didn't even notice that I had walked in, so I made a noise as if clearing my throat.

"Girl, you scared me. I didn't even know you had walked this way."

I just stared at him.

"Why you looking at me like that?"

"I could look at you however I want."

"Sound like you have an attitude. What did I do now?"

"How about you tell me what you did, Mark?"

"I ain't doing nothing, so please don't start an argument."

"I'm tired of these childish games you playing. You need to let me know what is going on and be honest."

He kept playing dumb as if he didn't know what I was talking about, and that made me even madder.

I looked him dead in his eyes without a glimpse of a smirk. "So who is the bitch texting your phone, talking about she broke up with her man and if you are going to break up with me? Clearly y'all had to discuss the issues we were having for her to even ask such a thing. So are y'all planning on being together? Because, if so, you need to let me know, so I can get the fuck out of here."

"I don't know where this is coming from, and whoever told you this crap is lying."

"Didn't nobody have to tell me nothing! I seen in your damn phone, so stop lying! Next time you trying to do some sneaky shit, make sure you keep your phone on you and let your hoes know when you busy. I said but you know what I'm sick of this and I don't have time for this, I'm too good of a woman to be putting on up with this mess.

First of all why are you even going through my phone, and

I responded saying that are you trying to validate yourself, for one I didn't go through your phone, the damn messages pop up on the top of the screen without going through the phone so miss me with that crap.

So he gone say why you overreacting that ain't nothing but one of my homegirls it ain't nothing like that, I said Mark save that lie for somebody else, we been together two years and all of sudden this homegirl pop up?? Really? Stop lying because you pissing me off even more. I walked out the kitchen toward his room and began packing my clothes back in bag so I could go home because I was so hurt, and I couldn't stand to look him in his face.

He came behind me in the room saying you aren't going anywhere and stop acting like this.

I looked at him and gave him the hardest mean mug I could possibly make, and told him, Mark, this isn't the time, you need to seriously just back away.

He gone say you not leaving Megan, and he came behind me and began hugging me, and I kept trying to push him off me because I was so angry.

Baby, you are overreacting. Nobody will ever take your place, and it's no way in the hell I would leave you, so stop acting like this.

I told him I don't believe you at all and I have put too much of my time and effort in this relationship to be dwelling with crap. If you wanted to talk to other girls, you should've had this out of your system before we got in a relationship. I just sat on the bed and put my head down and put my hands over my face because I was so disgusted, and I was trying to keep myself from crying in front of him. I didn't want him to see me at my weak point.

He came beside me along the bed and put his arm around me, and said we can work through this and I promise things aren't as if they seem. He said let's go to the movies and let the night play out as it should.

I looked at him with disgust and told him to move as I went to grab my shoes to put on.

Mark kind of had a smirk on his face and said I love you, babe.

, and I just looked at him and rolled my eyes. I told him don't push because I really didn't want to go, but in my mind at the same time I was too tired to drive myself to my mom house so I was trying to stick it out through the night.

He and I went to the movies, I had let go of my attitude somewhat, and it was extremely cold in the theater. He knew I was cold so he wrapped his arm around me, but I nudged and jerked back from him. I mean, I was really pissed.

He whispered in my ear, "Really, Megan, this is how we are going to act?"

I just looked him and rolled my eyes.

"We could've stayed at the house if you were going to act like this."

"We sure could have, but you kept on insisting that we come."

He took a deep breath and insisted that he was going to wrap his arm around me. So after of a couple of times of resistant I finally gave in.

After the movie had ended we went back to his apartment, and I ran in the house got in the shower and got in the bed and told him not to touch me. But of course, you know that didn't happen instead I gave in once again and allowed him to have a sexual encounter with me because I wanted it just as bad as he did.

As we woke up the next morning, he and I discussed the issue that had happened the previous night, and I told him that make it the last time he slip up in this relationship because I don't have time for the drama nor the excessive lies. I left his apartment and went to visit my family and friends.

After finding out about the chick texting his phone, honestly no I didn't trust him not one bit, but at the same time my love for him never faded. So I kept hope in what looked like a hopeless situation.

Mark and I continued to work on our relationship, and it was pretty tough because he was in Mississippi and I was in Alabama, about three and half hours away from each another. He started back calling more, like when we'd first started dating, but he still kept going out of town continuously with his friends. But, hey, I had eventually gotten used to that. It seemed as though that wasn't going to change, no matter how much I fussed.

He eventually became more serious about moving to Alabama with me. So each day he would get email notifications to his phone about hospital careers within the area I stayed so he could move.

At this point, I felt like I was finally getting the Mark I wanted and longed for this entire time. Not only was he thinking about moving, but he was thinking about marriage too. I was like, I would take his flaws, and we could work on this together as if I was just the perfect person.

I began helping him apply for jobs, but he had to become certified in the state of Alabama before applying for some jobs in order to get hired. I gave him the information he needed to take the exam and get the licensure, but he either kept putting the test off or would find a lame excuse. At one point, he wanted to change careers and begin working offshore. So he was just all over the place, but yet and still I was in his corner supporting him in whatever journey he wanted to take.

One Sunday morning Mark and I were talking on the phone before we both went to church. We would always send pictures of ourselves to one another every Sunday morning. I don't know why we did on Sundays, but that was just a habit we had.

On this particular Sunday morning, he sent me the picture to my email but I didn't think to look at the picture till after I got out of church service when I made it back to my apartment. Mark kept calling me after church

"Have you looked at the picture I sent"

"No, not yet, I haven't had a chance to take a look because I went to church and I had to run some errand"

While we were on the phone, he continuously kept asking, "Have you looked yet."

Finally, I opened the email up and took a look at the picture,

"Babe you look good, who were you trying to look good for at church" in a joking manner, and Laughing "Baby this for you and only you
"

We both chuckled.

"I am about to start cooking, I will call you back once I'm done",

"Why you can't cook and talk on the phone with me"

"Babe when I cook do I ever talk on the phone?"

Mark become silent over the phone with a long pause

"As soon as I finish cooking I promise I will call you back."

It was very odd that Mark was trying to cling to me on the phone, but I thought, maybe he really misses me.

As I went to the bathroom, I always take my phone with me because I usually read while I'm in the bathroom, call me weird but hey that's just me. Something in the back of my mind said Megan go back to that email that Mark sent. I went back to take a look at the email and I clicked the CC: button the email sender portion, and it was some other chick's email in the address log. It was like I could feel the ecstasy coming out of me, I was like we just had a discussion about this bull crap and here he goes again.

So before I said anything to him, I emailed the chick and asked her who she was and why was Mark sending her the pictures. Within seconds, she emailed me back, stating that she and Mark were friends and they had been talking for about three months. I wrote her back saying, WELL, HONEY, YOU MUST BE MISTAKEN BECAUSE MARK HAS BEEN IN A RELATIONSHIP WITH ME FOR TWO AND A HALF YEARS.

She wrote me back apologetically saying that she didn't know that he was in a relationship, and when she asked him did he have a girlfriend he denied, saying he wasn't in a relationship, and they meet in New Orleans and from there they would meet up to see one another from time to time.

So by then a lot of stuff started adding up in my mind. First, I assumed this was the same chick that had texted his phone the day I was at his house. Second, while he was telling me his homeboys were messing with random chicks down in New Orleans, he was doing the same damn thing. Third, how do you make time to go see another chick in New Orleans, but you complain continuously about driving to Alabama to come see your girlfriend?

After getting all this valid information from her. I called Mark

"Why did you keep asking me to check my email"

"I was just asking out of curiosity, dang"

"Really! Mark stop trying to play me like some idiot. If you are going to continue to cheat, please be much smarter, the dumb ass moves you are making clearly aren't working because you get caught every time"

"For one why would you email two girls the same picture? What? You thought because it was CC, I wouldn't see it. Stop being so damn dumb. Tell me who this chick is"

"She one my home girls from San Antonio and I hadn't seen her in a while and we were catching up"

"Bitch, stop lying so much and tell me the truth, and this situation would be so much easier"

"I'm serious"

"More so seriously lying"

"I already have talked to her and she has told me a mouthful and she doesn't have a reason to lie"

He began yelling horrendously "Why did you email her, you didn't have no place in writing her all this is going to do is start some mess"

"Don't try to flip the script on me because if I were in the same vicinity as you I would slap the crap out of you, so please don't even cross that line with me"

He immediately hung up the phone in my face, so I called him back and

"You scared to tell me the truth. I said just be honest and tell me what is going on"

"Baby I apologize I know I messed up"

"Yeah you sure did, but I want to know if everything she saying is true"

"I don't want to talk about it right now"

"You don't have a choice but to talk about it right now because it is an issue right now, and I'm about done with this relationship on everything I love"

"Let me explain I'm just hurting because I know I hurt you"

I said whatever Mark and hung up the phone with him because I had no more words for him at all. So he kept calling and calling, and I wouldn't answer.

At this point, I didn't know what to think nor what to say. I was hurt, I shedding tears because I couldn't understand how you could love a person so much, but they continuously found ways to manipulate and hurt you. I knew deep down that I couldn't allow myself to go down this same ole dead end road. Yes, I cried tremendously my heart was broke, but I knew I needed to pull myself together because I was much stronger than my circumstance.

God spoke to me and told me I was putting more effort into man than into Him. I saw myself shun away from God, and not giving Him my all as I should, yes I was going to church, yes I was paying my tithes and offerings, but I wasn't reading my Bible and spending quality time with Him as I should. And this happening was a reflection of my ignorance of God.

So I fell on my knees and asked God to forgive me for neglecting Him, and he said, daughter, you have been forgiven. As I remember my pastor saying Jesus is in love with the backsliders and I knew I had backslidden from Christ, so it was time for me to do some re-evaluating of my life.

Finally, I picked up the phone to call Mark back, and he answered all quietly as if scared,

"Hello"

In my dry monotone voice "What's up"

"I'm ready to talk but let me first start off by saying I'm genuinely sorry, and I know I took advantage of you, and I don't want to lose you but if you leave me I truly understand but I screwed this up, but I will do anything in my power to keep you"

After hearing that spell, I was like blah blah, of course, you want to let out all your feelings at this point.

"I'm listening"

"Yes she and I were talking but it wasn't on the status as a relationship, but she did know I had a girlfriend so she was lying about that part, we only seen each other once outside of New Orleans, but we meet halfway"

I felt myself becoming sorrowful for myself inside, but I was wiping away tears as they came.

So I asked him, "Did y'all have sexual encounters?"

There was a long pause over the phone.

"Mark, answer me. Did y'all have sexual encounters?"

"Yes, but it was only once."

After hearing that, I couldn't hold my composure. I burst out in tears.

"I'm done, I can't with you, how could you have sex with someone you didn't know… you are so nasty and I don't even know you as a person anymore"

This was my breaking point that I needed to go the doctor asap because he was having sex with she and I. I told him at this point you not only didn't have respect for me but for yourself as well because you don't even know this chick and you around here having sex with her.

He said I didn't have unprotected sex with her,

I told him that didn't matter, and the love he claims he had for me was all a lie.

Megan, don't act like you perfect and you have never done wrong.

"First of all I never said I was perfect and secondly this isn't about me, and he needed to accept his faults and the damage his brought in this relationship"

"When we first started dating you had some football player texting your phone one and two o'clock in the morning, I could have easily thought that something was going on"

"You did think something, but I told you I can call the guy up and he can tell you himself we had nothing going on during the point of time you and I got together, the guy even admitted he was drunk when he called me and it was by mistake, so you can miss me with the unnecessary drama"

"You know what better yet, we can end this discussion"

"Clearly I'm not what you want. Maybe I'm what you need but you're not appreciative and I'm tired of supporting someone who is taking me for granted. All the open opportunities I had to cheat, did I do it? "

"How would I know, I'm not with you all the time"

"NO! Because, at the end of the day, I was respectful of your feelings, and I had enough pride and sense about myself. If I wanted to run the streets, I would be up front and honest with you. at this point I can no longer drag myself in this race with you because there will always be competition with the unknown"

I hung up in his face once again.

About ten minutes later his mom called, and she and I had a pretty close bond, and she and I shared some personal things amongst one another. So when she called,

I answered with an attitude,

"What's wrong"

"Nothing at all" *in a rudely tone*

"Well it sound as though something is wrong"

And in that instance I burst out in tears,

" Megan are you all right, what is going on,

So I went on with the notion of telling her that Mark had cheated on me with some girl he met in New Orleans that was from Texas, and not only did he cheat but he had sex with her, and I felt so unworthy, nasty, and disgusted. I told her that I could no longer carry on a relationship with her son because I was too young to be going through all this with someone his age, it would be different if we were the same age or he was younger but he was five years older so this is unacceptable.

"Megan I can't believe this. I don't know why he go out and do something like this. You are a strong lady and you have been very faithful to him and his daughter, and you don't deserve that type of treatment"

She kept telling me to stop crying and remain strong,

I told her I was at my breaking point, and I could no longer hold it end. I told her I felt as though someone had come in and just stomped on my heart, and I told her I should have known something was going on, but I was so foolish I didn't see it coming.

"Stop blaming yourself for what happened.

I told her, all this could have been avoided if I'd just paid attention to the warning signs.

She said let me go talk to him, and in the meantime you stay calm and relax.

I told her she didn't have to talk to him about it because I was completely done with him, and I no longer wanted to be with him.

I had cried so much, I cried myself to sleep. That was some serious shedding of tears, I tell you.

I woke up to a lot of text messages and two missed calls, one from Mark, the other from his mom, but all the text messages were from Mark. I didn't even bother to look at the text messages, just for the simple fact I didn't want to even read what he had to say.

I called his mom back, and she asked me was I all right, I told her yea I was fine, and I could make it through this, and she said well I tried to talk to him but he just shut everybody because he knew he was wrong, and he didn't want to discuss anything.

So late that night, I decided to call him back and I asked him what did he want.

"Can you just allow me to explain?"

In a nonchalant voice "Yes, but make it quick because I'm ready to go to bed."

"I love you with all my heart. I know you probably don't believe me. I take the blame for all that. I know you aren't going to trust and forgive me overnight, but I do pray you give me an opportunity to prove to you that I can be the man you prayed for. I can't imagine living a day without, and I need you in my life. Not only have I hurt you, but this will affect my daughter as well because I know the bond you all have with one another. That would hurt her, you are not being a part of our life. I can't take back what I have done, but I can try to make up for what I have done. If you don't want to be with me, I can understand that. Even though it would hurt, I would have to merely respect your decision and live with it"

"You have a successful career, you're financially stable, spiritual, and you have a drive about yourself, so you would make the perfect woman for any man, but I want you to be that woman for me."

"Let me think on it because honestly, Mark, I don't know if I want this relationship anymore. Instead of adding happiness in my life, it's putting more stress on me. This isn't what I desired of relationship. If we were to get back together, I wouldn't trust you at all, and it would take an extremely long time to gain that trust back. And I don't know if you're willing to put up with that"

Baby I understand and I'm willing to do whatever to please you.

We will see, but I'm getting ready for bed so I will holla at you when I do.

Really? Well, I love you.

I said mm-hmm, and I hung up the phone.

Seconds later I received a text message: SO YOU CAN'T SAY I LOVE YOU

I texted back: NO

He replied back: OKAY I CAN TAKE THAT

I played back and forth in my mind if I were going to give Mark another chance. Deep down in my heart I truly loved him, and if anyone has fell in love they know it is hard to just completely stop loving someone. I was so heartbroken that as I lay in the bed all I could do was cry my eyes out. I cried so much, I had no more tears to spare. I just went into a deep huffing and puffing.

After about three hours of crying, I finally made myself go to sleep. In the back of my head, I remembered my pastor saying, "Tears don't move God, prayer moves God."

I stopped crying immediately and asked God to heal the pain in my heart and to give me the strength in order to forgive Mark.

When I found out Mark had betrayed me, it was about two weeks before Valentine's Day. So I within those weeks I toggled in my mind about my relationship with him, yes I wanted to be him, but was I truly going to be able to give my all stating that I knew for a fact that I didn't trust him whatsoever, and it would be a long time before I ever trusted him.

I continued to talk to Mark, and he kept asking me was I willing to put in the work toward our relationship, and I kept telling him let me think about it, I'm not sure because you have cut me deep this time, and I'm not sure if the try again is worth it.

I felt as though I could start over with someone much better rather than continuing to go back and forth with him, but I kept thinking about the good times he and I shared and should I really give him a shot at it again.

Valentine's Day rolled around and I woke up to a long video/media message from Mark, he had a song by Avant playing the background with him expressing himself and how he felt toward me, he said that he wanted to build a future, and he knew that God had placed me in his life for a lifetime, and he is willing to let go of his foolish and prideful ways to do whatever it takes to please me and make this relationship survive. It was sweet and as I was listening and reading the message I began to weep because I wanted to be happy and that moment to be special, but my heart wouldn't allow me to feel that way because I kept remembering the hurt, the cheating, the lying, the conniving, and the betrayal.

I said to myself why he couldn't be this way without the excessive pain that he has caused me. I mean I felt as though the message was genuine, but the timing was incorrect.

About midday at work, I received an email from the secretary telling me that something in the front had arrived, and I was wondering what this could be because I didn't remember ordering anything and having it shipped to the office, so I was like okay… with a confusing look.

When I made it to the front and saw a bouquet of roses and a card. By this point, I was trying to figure out who the heck could've sent me these flowers. They couldn't have been from Mark since he was all the way in Mississippi, and he had never given me flowers. In fact, he always used to say he wasn't the flower type of guy.

I opened the card it was a sweet innocent message from Mark: I KNEW THIS WOULD SURPRISE, YOU AND I WANT THIS RELATIONSHIP SO BAD I WILL DO THE THINGS THAT I SAID I WOULD NEVER DO JUST TO BE IN YOUR GOOD GRACE, I LOVE YOU BABE, AND THIS IS ONLY THE BEGINNING.

I was so shocked. My insides felt so warm, as I felt the heat flow from my toes to my head. I felt so loved. I couldn't even figure out how he got this done since I didn't give him my work address or anything.

Sitting at my desk looking at the roses, I thought, *Yes, it's worth giving this relationship a try. Since he is putting forth the effort, I should do the same in return.*

I called him and told him thank you and I loved the flowers, and he has proven somewhat that he wanted to change due to the more frequent visits, and fewer arguments. I had also noticed that he wasn't spending so much time with his boys.

I told him, "Yes, I will give this relationship another try. Do I trust you one hundred percent? No. Will it happen over time, someway, somehow? But I just don't know as of right now."

We both agreed that distance between us was hurting our relationship. Mark said that he was going to be more persistent with trying to find a job within in my area, while, at the same time, I was looking for a job back at home because I missed not only being with him but, more importantly, my family.

Over the course of the month, I applied for a job as a marketing database analyst and went for an interview. My faith was so strong in God, I began packing my clothes and furniture back in Alabama because I knew the job was mine, in the name of Jesus. The job was at the casino and was somewhat similar to the one I had in Alabama.

Within a week of the interview, I got the call back that the job was mine, and was paying me twice the amount my current job was paying. One of the perks about getting a job back at home was, I also gained the privilege of attending graduate school.

I immediately called Mark and told him that I had got the job.

He was so excited and happy, he said, "Baby, you just don't know how much stress this has taken off of me. Things can finally go back to normal."

"Yes, this is definitely what we need at this point for our relationship to survive."

Within two weeks, I moved back home. Our relationship was back on a high like when we'd first started dating. We began spending more time together, sometimes two to three nights a week. And I was spending more time with his daughter. It was my perfect "dream family" once again.

A Slight Detour

After receiving the job back at home, Mark and I were able to spend more time together, giving us an opportunity to restore our broken relationship. While things were going great, and we had the picture-perfect relationship again, deep down I still felt a sense of loneliness. Now don't get me wrong, Mark was taking me out dates, buying me lavish gifts, taking me on vacations, saying sweet things to me, but I still felt like something was missing.

I loved my job working at the casino as the marketing database manager because I was able to meet new people every day. During my time there, not a day went by that I didn't have a smile on my face from laughing and joking with coworkers and guests.

With me being the new chick at the casino, everybody was introducing themselves to me and trying to get to know me. Some of the guys there would make flirtatious remarks, but I would just laugh and kind of brush them off because I didn't have any interest in them. Of course, they were trying to feel me out, to see if it would be easy to get in bed with me. I wasn't that foolish.

One particular day after working there for about two months, I saw this guy working there that I hadn't seen before, so I just assumed he was new to the job. That week all new employees had an orientation that we were required to attend. I looked around the room and he wasn't there, so I thought maybe he wasn't new.

Two weeks went by, and I didn't see the guy at all. I mean, I couldn't miss him because he was a tall, handsome, light-skinned man. Just the sight of him made my day honestly.

It was about a month later when I saw him walking toward the cage, and he gave me a smile and wink. Boy, I could have passed out and hit the floor. I had on a fitted black and white dress with my black pumps, and I gave him one of those over-the-shoulder hellos as if I wasn't really paying him any attention. I looked at the badge on his shirt and realized he worked for an outside company the casino, which explained why I didn't see him all the time.

So as I was walking the casino floor, he came up to me and said, "Hey, you must be new because I haven't seen you around here before."

I told him, "Yes, I'm somewhat new. I've been here for about two months now.'

"Oh, okay. Well, I hope to see you more often.'

I laughed and walked off with no response. As I walked off, I could feel him staring at me, but I didn't want to give him too much attention, because for one, I had a boyfriend, and two, I wanted him to work hard to try to get at me.

About a week later, I got a call from the front desk in my office saying that someone wanted to see me up front.

The first thing I thought was, *Dang! What guest is complaining now about the points or offers they received in the mail?* I was really busy and didn't have time to acknowledge that issue at that point in time. So I asked the clerk, "Who is it?"

She said, "Some guy."

"What guy?"

"I'm not sure who he is, but he asked to see you."

So I said in a slow voice, "Well, okay … I will be up there in a second."

While I was sitting at my desk finishing up typing an email before I walked to the floor, I was wondering who in the heck could this be. I knew for sure it wasn't Mark because I'd stayed with him the night before, and we left the house at the same time to go to the apartment. And I know it wasn't my dad because the clerk would've just outright said so.

After I sent off the email and straightened my clothes and made sure my makeup and hair were all put together, I walked slowly up to the front. I made it to the clerk's desk and didn't see anyone standing up there waiting for me.

I asked, "Who's looking for me?"

The clerk said, "He's on the floor walking around."

"I thought you said it wasn't a guest that was asking for me."

"He isn't. He's an outside contractor or vendor for us."

So I was like, "Why in the heck do they want to talk to me? I don't handle any of that crap."

She said, "Just wait right here. Let me go get him."

I breathed really hard. "Okay, please go ahead because I have a lot to do before twelve o clock."

I was leaning over on the clerk's desk checking emails on my cell phone when she came back, and lo and behold, it was that fine guy I had been eyeing. He had the nerve to have her call and find me so we could talk.

He came up and said, "Hi, Megan."

I said, "Hello" in my very professional voice. "Is there something you would like me to help you with?"

He said, "As a matter of fact, yes. That's why I had this young lady call you from your office. Do you have a minute to talk?"

"Literally only a minute. It's pretty hectic around here."

"Okay, I won't hold you long."

Because I wasn't sure what he was going to say was appropriate for the clerk to hear, I told him, "Let's walk to the side and talk."

"Ever since the last time I laid my eyes on you, I've been trying to figure out who you were."

I laughed. "Hmm. Oh really. What made you so curious to figure out who I was?"

"You have an aura about yourself that's different from the other women around here." Larry looked me up and down.

I said, "First of all, sir, what is your name? Because you never told me your name."

"I do apologize for that. My name is Larry. Would there be any chance of me getting to know you as a person outside of the work facility?"

"Hmmmm. I don't think that is possible. I've been in a relationship for about three years, and I'm not looking for anybody."

He said, "I apologize. I should've known someone of your character and intelligence was in a committed relationship."

At that moment, I had a flashback of all the hurtful things Mark had done to me. I remember thinking, *I could react in this moment and pay him back for all the things he did to me*, but I didn't even want to deal with that drama, and I was too mature of a person to even stoop that low.

I told him, "Well, it was nice meeting you, Larry. I will see you around."

"Yep. Hope to see you sooner than later," he said, and he shook my hand and placed his business card in my hand with his phone number." He added, "Now the ball is in your court. Hit me up when you're ready."

I kind of slightly rolled my eyes because I didn't want any further relations with him.

* * *

When I stayed in Alabama, I went to the gym about three to four days a week to stay in shape; it was also a way for me to release stress. I decided to continue to work out when I moved back home and started going to the local community gym.

One day I was walking in the gym, I seen Larry from across the gym walking toward the entrance as well. And, oh my goodness, he body outside his work attire was horrendous, he had muscles popping out of every seam in that shirt, his calf muscles looked like mountains. So I tried to look in my car side mirror to make sure my ponytail was somewhat on point. Part of me wanted to run in the gym and try to avoid him while at the same time I wanted to walk slow so he could approach me because that man right there was one of America's finest, I tell you.

I had to remember at the same time think about how Mark would feel, but hey what he didn't know wouldn't hurt him, and all I was about to do was have a casual conversation.

Before I could make up my mind what I wanted to do, Larry hollered across the parking lot, "What's up, Megan?"

I turned around and acted as if I didn't know who was speaking and threw my hand up in the air.

He ran over across the parking lot, and said, "You act like you didn't know who I was."

I said, "Boy, I can't see that far. All I heard was Megan."

"Mm-hmm. Don't try to play hard."

I laughed because this guy knew the kind of game I was trying to play.

As we were walking to the gym together, he said with an ironic tone, "Well, how have you been doing? Since I haven't heard from you."

I told him, "What did I tell you?—I can't be calling or texting you while I'm in a relationship."

"I guess, but whatever. How you been?"

"Things have been going great. Yourself?"

"Pretty good. Can't complain."

"Now I know when you're right."

He laughed. "You are so different," he said. "I just can pinpoint it out."

"How can you say something is different about me when you don't even know me?"

"I just know and keep it like that."

I turned my lip upward and to side and said, "I guess if you say so."

As we were talking, I kept trying to look forward because my eyes were engaging in all the wrong places. In this particular gym, there was a side for women, and a side for men and women, and I always went to the women side.

When we made it to the entrance, I said, "I will see you later."

He said, "I will holla at you."

I smiled and kind of switched as I walked off. I had to make this man never forget me.

* * *

I stayed in the gym for about an hour. I was going to stay the night with Mark.

As I walked out, I had my head down, texting on my phone. I heard somebody say, "Pick your head up before you trip up."

I looked up, and of course, it was Larry, laughing.

I said, "Whatever. You think you got jokes."

"N'all. I was just messing around with you." Then he asked, "What are your plans after gym?"

I told him, "I'm rushing to get to my boyfriend's house to have dinner prepared for him when he gets off."

"That is sweet of you."

"They say the closer you get to a man's heart, the more you feed him."

"Well, let me back up," he said, putting his hands up in mock surrender. "I don't want homeboy to run up on me over here talking to you."

"You have nothing to worry about. He lives about an hour away."

"Oh wow!" he said with a big grin.

"Why are you smiling so hard? Just because we don't live in the same town don't mean I'm going to be sneaky at all."

Larry said, "I wasn't even thinking that way. You must have those intentions in mind."

I was at a loss for words because those thoughts did run through my head, but I wasn't going to act out on them.

He said, "How about this? You just give me one hour of conversation one day as friends, and if you can't handle that, I promise I will just leave you alone altogether. All I want is one chance."

"Let me think about that."

"Man, you ain't gone do nothing."

I laughed hilariously. "For real, let me think about it and get back with you."

As I was walking to the car, he said, "I'm going to be waiting on that text or call from you soon."

I laughed and threw my hands in the air at him.

When I got in the car, I called up my Ash. I had to give her the 411. For real!!!

I said, "Girl, you know that guy I was telling you about some weeks ago? I just saw him at the gym, and that nigga is fine as hell, girl! My flesh was wanting to give in and hand him my number, but I kept thinking about how bad I would hurt Mark in the end."

She said, "Well, you did the right thing."

"No, I didn't. He wants to meet up with me one day during the week and have a conversation over dinner."

"So basically he wants to take you out on a date."

"No, not necessarily. We would just talk over dinner as friends like you and I would do.

Ash burst out laughing. "Girl, you can think that if you want to, but that man trying to get to your heart and in your head."

I was like, "But I'm strong enough to not let it go there like seriously, come on this your girl Megan. You know I put the *faith* in faithful. Look at my middle name—La'Faith."

She cracked up laughing, saying, "Girl, you a fool. I can't deal with you."

"For real, I'm thinking about texting him and taking him up on his offer. It's just something about him that attracts me beyond his looks. I ain't gon' lie—that nigga clean as a whistle and smoother than a baby's butt."

"Look at you," she said, "already jumping in your feelings."

"It's no way I'm jumping in my feelings for the simple fact I'm in love with my baby Mark."

"You might be in love, but you have an interest in Larry. Make up your mind and do what you want to do. I have your back one hundred percent."

"That's all ya girl wanted to hear."

We laughed and hung up on the phone.

As I was driving down the road heading to Mark's house, I decided to shoot Larry a text.

He responded back within seconds: MAN I'M SHOCKED YOU TEXT ME, I REALLY THOUGHT I DIDN'T STAND A CHANCE WITH YOU AT ALL

I texted: WELL WE JUST COOL FRIENDS SO HEY WHATS THE BIG DEAL

YOU RIGHT I AIN'T TRYING TO TAKE YOUR MAN PLACE AT ALL, BUT JUST MAKE SURE HE DON'T SLIP UP

YOU HAVE NO WORRIES ABOUT THAT AT ALL

I HOPE YOU'RE NOT TEXTING AND DRIVING

YEP THAT'S WHAT I'M DOING

Next thing I know, my phone began ringing. Larry was calling me. I answered, and he said, "I don't want you to risk your life texting me while driving. I rather you talk on the phone. That way you can use your hands-free Bluetooth in your car."

That shocked me that he considered and cared for me enough to not risk me texting him. He didn't know, but that was a turn-on to me.

We were talking about life and the goals we wanted to achieve and how we were going to reach those goals. He told me about his past relationship, and how he and his past girlfriend were having issues, but they still conversed from time to time, but he didn't think that being in a relationship was best for the two of them.

So I went on telling him about Mark and my relational issues but I have forgiven him and I thought it was worth a second try with because I truly loved and wanted to be with him.

He said, "Well, I definitely respect you for giving your all in a relationship." Then he added, "But don't let your worth and value decrease for the satisfaction of someone else. And that not only pertains to intimate relationships but with family and friends as well."

"So true."

Before I knew it, I had made it to Mark's apartment and was still on the phone with Larry. I couldn't believe we had talked the entire way to my destination. I told him I had made it to Mark's house and would talk to him tomorrow evening.

Larry said, "How about we talk over dinner tomorrow?"

I told him, "Sure. Just text me the details."

After hanging up the phone with Larry, I just sat in the car and began thinking about the encouraging advice he gave me about my relationship. Which was shocking. I was expecting him to try to lure me away from Mark rather than toward him.

Call me crazy, but I was kind of falling for Larry because his personality was out of this world.

As I was just sitting in the car thinking, Mark came out the house and knocked on the car window. "What are you doing?" he asked. "Why are you just sitting in the car?"

"I'm coming in. I was trying to get my stuff together in the car."

So he opened the back door and got my bags, and I got out of the car. As I was walking behind him, I just shook my head with a slick grin, thinking, *If only he knows what's really going on.*

As Mark and I were talking, it was like everything he was saying was going through one ear and out the other. I was preoccupied with Larry. I was like, *Dang, everything I've been looking for in years with Mark, it seems as though I found in an hour conversation with Larry.* But I had to remember not to let myself get too deep because Mark was the man I wanted to be with; plus, I had invested so much time and effort.

When Mark and I went to bed, I would usually put my phone on the charger next to him, but this particular night I decided to let my phone charge in the living area, just in case Larry decided he wanted to text or call. I didn't want any drama.

The next morning when I woke up, I ran to the living room to get my phone to see if Larry had texted me, but he didn't. I felt a certain type of way, but maybe he was just trying to be respectful, knowing I was at my boyfriend's house.

Mark said, "You woke up early this morning."

"Yeah," I said, "I have to hurry and get to work."

"Why?"

I told him, "I have a lot of work to catch up on."

* * *

The next day rolled around, and Larry invited me to a nice little restaurant downtown, saying we could meet up around seven. This was perfect because it gave me enough time to talk to Mark and kind of fend him off for a while.

I told Mark that my best friend and I were having us a girls' night, and I would call him when I was heading home, and he was fine with that.

So I met up with Larry, and we talked and laughed all night until it was time for the restaurant to close.

Leaving the restaurant, he walked me to car and said, "I really enjoyed this night out with you. You are a really genuine and kindhearted woman. Even though you have been misused emotionally, you are still able to have a positive view on life, and I commend you on that."

I was so amazed, I didn't even have words to say to him. I told him, "That's one of the kindest things I've heard in years."

He said, "As your friend, that's what I'm supposed to do."

I laughed flirtatiously, and he gave me a hug and whispered in my ear, "Hopefully I get this opportunity more often."

"We'll see about that."

I watched Larry walk to his car and said out loud to myself, "What have I gotten myself into?" I was really feeling this dude on a serious level.

Driving home, I was just thinking about how much we talked as if we'd known each other for years. Larry was the man I longed for, but at the same time I knew I couldn't allow this to happen.

I called Mark just out of respect, but the conversation was dry because my mind wasn't on him at all.

As time went on, it got to the point where Larry and I were going either to the gym or to the high school stadium to work out together about two to three days a week. He knew I was still with Mark and didn't have any intention of breaking up with him.

At the same time, I still didn't want to lose my friendship with Larry. I would continuously ask him was he okay with me having a boyfriend, and did it bother him. He would always tell me no because he knew I was in a relationship before he pursued the friendship with me.

Well, one day he and I were walking around the track, and I tripped on a crack in the gravel and hurt my ankle. He picked me up off my feet, but I insisted that he put me down.

He said, "No, no, no. You look like you are really hurting." So he carried me to my car and sat me in the driver's seat. He told me, "Let me see your ankle."

I slid my leg into his hand, and he gently rubbed his hand up and down my leg and around my ankle. As he touched me, my body became tense.

He looked at me and told me, "Chill out and calm down."

I asked him, "What are you talking about?"

He gave me a knowing look.

"What?"

He replied, "Nothing at all, Megan," and he began laughing.

I told him, "I'd be all right," and I pulled my leg back from him, feeling like it was a bit inappropriate. Even though, it felt really good, I knew it wasn't the right thing to do. I said, "Thank you. I need to get back home because I don't want Mark to notice a change in my schedule and start questioning me."

I knew I needed to pull back from Larry, but it was like a part of me just couldn't let go. I had become so attached to his conversation and company, it was almost as though he was taking the place of Mark.

One evening Larry and I were together talking and laughing, and he grabbed me by my waist and hugged me, and before I knew it, I reached in for a kiss from him. I couldn't believe that I'd done that.

We looked at each other kind of sheepishly, and I told him hurriedly, "I need to go home," and quickly walked away without addressing what had happened.

As I walked off, he said, "Wait, Megan. Let's talk."

I threw my hands in the air and never looked back. When I got in my car, Mark was calling me. I couldn't even answer the phone because I knew I would sound guilty. I just sat and let the phone ring.

I was thinking to myself, *Why did I let things get so deep so quickly?* All this happened within the span of a month.

After I made it home, I was on the phone with Mark for about thirty minutes. He kept asking me, "Is something wrong?" since I wasn't saying much on the phone.

"No. I'm just tired from work."

"Okay, so I will let you get some rest. Just call me when you wake up."

While I was on the phone with Mark, Larry had sent me a two-page text message, but I waited until I got off the phone to read it. I APOLOGIZE FOR WHAT HAPPENED AND I NEVER MEANT FOR IT TO GO THAT FAR. I KNOW THE ATTRACTION BETWEEN US IS GROWING DEEPLY. I UNDERSTAND IF YOU WANT TO PULL BACK

After reading the message, I replied: IT WASN'T TOTALLY YOUR FAULT. I PLAYED A PART IN WHAT HAPPENED. AND I REACTED IN A CHILDISH MANNER

I decided to pick up the phone and call him because I genuinely enjoyed the friendship he and I shared, and I didn't want to lose that. We both decided that we needed to slow things down, and only remain friends.

About two months had passed, and Larry and I were strictly on a platonic level. One Tuesday evening he invited me to go out to dinner with him at a new restaurant over in Louisiana., This particular day Mark had decided he wanted to go see his hometown team play at a basketball tournament, so I had some free time.

Larry and I went to this nice mid-upscale restaurant, and we laughed and talked about everything under the sun. As we talked, I could feel the attraction growing stronger between us. I think in a way I was starting to love Larry more than I loved Mark.

As we were riding back to Vicksburg, Larry looked at me and said, "You are an amazing person, you know that?"

I told him, "You are too. That's why you're my bestie," and we both laughed.

We were riding and singing together, and I was just really enjoying myself.

We made it back to town and stopped at his house so I could get my car. When we got there, I had to use the bathroom, so he invited me in. This was my very first time going in his home.

When I came out the bathroom, I saw a picture of him at a pro game, and we had a discussion about our favorite teams.

Before I knew it, I had plopped my butt on the couch, and he and I were watching a movie together.

I told him that I was about to go because I needed to get home, and he said, "N'all. You just know you gon' get in trouble if you don't answer that phone."

"Whatever. That doesn't have anything to do with it," I said when I knew deep down that was exactly the issue.

He reached out and gave me a long hug, and we looked each other in the eyes. We both reached in and kissed each other, but this time I didn't pull back.

Larry pulled back and started laughing. He said, "I knew you wanted me just as bad as I wanted you."

I laughed. "N'all. You want me way more."

So we began kissing even more, which led us to the bedroom, where we had our first sexual encounter.

While we were having sex, not one time did I think about Mark. I knew it wasn't right, but at that moment, there was nowhere else I wanted to be.

After we had our affair, I left, and when I got on the car, I began crying because I knew what I was doing wasn't right. But my heart was in so deep, I felt trapped.

When I made it home, I told Larry that things went way farther than I'd intended. I went to the bathroom to run my bath water, and as I turned around and looked at myself in the mirror, I saw an unpleasant, disgusting, devious person.

I fell to my knees and asked God for forgiveness because I knew what I did was ungodly. I prayed that God release the soul tie on me because I'd seen a change in myself that I didn't like at all. I could see the burdens on my life, and the dead skin lying on my body from my ill-mannered acts. At that point, I realized the seriousness of soul ties and how they are able to control your life.

The Bible in 1 Corinthians 6:16-20 states: There's more to sex than mere skin on skin. Sex is as much spiritual mystery as physical fact. As written in Scripture, "The two become one." Since we want to become spiritually one with the Master, we must not pursue the kind of sex that avoids commitment and intimacy, leaving us more lonely than ever—the kind of sex that can never "become one." There is a sense in which sexual sins are different from all others. In sexual sin, we violate the sacredness of our own bodies, these bodies that were made for God-given and God-modeled love, for "becoming one" with another. Or didn't you realize that your body is a sacred place, the place of the Holy Spirit? Don't you see that you can't live however you please, squandering what God paid such a high price for? The physical part of you is not some piece of property belonging to the spiritual part of you. God owns the whole works. So let people see God in and through your body.

Feeling disgusted with myself, I asked God to send me signs and wonders of wisdom, because this was a spirit I wasn't fighting against.

I remember going to church the following Sunday and hearing my bishop say, "In today's era, we aren't fighting against flesh and blood but against spiritual wickedness in high places."

I knew that message was for me.

He added, "You can't fist-fight your way out, but you have to give God total control and just pray and press your way through."

That was my cue to leave Larry alone. The enemy was using him to get to me off track because he knew the desires that God had in store for me. I learned at that point what looks good, smells good, and talks good ain't always a good thing. You dress a person up the right way and they will fool you like a wolf in sheep clothing.

After arriving home from church that Sunday, I called Larry and told him that we would need to seriously stop talking, that I had to let go of our friendship because I saw myself going down the wrong path.

He said, "Well, you act as if it was all me."

I responded, "It isn't all you at all. I should have stopped this in the beginning, knowing deep down that it would go farther than I intended." Then I added, "If I hurt you in any way, shape, or form, or you feel manipulated, I truly apologize, but having these relations with you is not going to continue to happen because I'm not strong enough mentally to avoid the temptation."

Naturally, he didn't want to end the friendship, and he began saying unkind things to me.

I told him, "I respect you, and I would never get out of character with you, but it is what it is. I am done." And I politely hung up the phone in his face and never looked back again.

Oops, I Did It

Mark and I worked on rebuilding and rekindling our relationship, and I was giving him all of me wholeheartedly because he was the one I wanted to spend the rest of my life with. He and I had talked about marriage on numerous occasions, and we were basically planning our life out together. Like a big part of me felt like I owed Mark due to the fact that I was cheating even though I never got caught I still felt guilty. So I was just giving him my all from heart to my time. After working at the casino for about seven months, I knew that job wasn't for me even though the pay was great, the environment was unhealthy and I was exposed to a lot of things that were more so hurtful in my walk of life rather than helpful. I reached out to my previous boss and he was willing to rehire me for my position I held in Alabama, and not only did he give me my job back, but he also allowed me the ability to work from home in Mississippi and travel to Alabama one week out of every month. I mean couldn't have asked for a better job; I mean God had placed some mega favor on my life.

I had just started my job around March, and this was my first time travelling back to Alabama since I had left, and they paid for me a hotel room with food accommodations. This particular evening after getting off from work, I didn't feel like going out having a sit down dinner, so I decided to grab a pizza from Domino's and head back to the room so I could get some rest, but as I was eating I was having some strange abdominal craps, and I had realized that my cycle hadn't come on within the past two days, but I was on the birth control shot so that made my cycle irregular. In my mind, I wasn't worried but at the same time I was somewhat concerned.

So I got up and ran to Walmart to get a pregnancy test, and I got the real legit test "First Choice" and there were two in the pack. When I was walking to the cash register, I kind of hid the test behind my purse because I didn't want people looking at me throughout the store with the pregnancy exam because people are so judgmental. When I made it to the register I kept my head down the whole time in embarrassment, you would've thought I was a fourteen-year-old going to buy a pregnancy test.

When I made it back to the hotel, I swung the door open, ran to the bathroom, ripped the box apart anxiously trying to get the pregnancy test out, and I sat and stared at the test, and said here we go all for nothing. So after urinating on the stick, I went back to the bed and began eating my pizza and watching *Love and Hip Hop*, I got some in tuned into the show that I forgot that I had even taken the test. After about thirty minutes, I ran back to the bathroom, and my heart dropped to my feet when I seen the results.

Lying on the bathroom floor in a puddle of tears, with a screeching voice of crying mixed with anger. I felt a shiver move up my back, but yet I was so tense, I couldn't move my body. At that boiling point, I knew that the reality of embracing the unknown was going to part of my lifestyle for the continuous years. As my eyes pondered back on the positive lines on the pregnancy test, my mind began to wonder, *What am I to do now?* I had received a promotion with my job and I was able to travel monthly and my relationship with God was on the right path. But just within seconds, I saw all that success just splatter before my eyes into a reality I wasn't ready to accept.

After Laying my head on the side of the toilet with a face drenching in tears of despair, I found a way to pull myself together to get up to go back in the hotel bedroom. I walked slowly and remorseful back to the bed and slid to my phone to call a dear friend of mine to tell her the news. Before I called her, I had to calm myself so she wouldn't hear the fear and shame in my voice. My voice was still trembling, but I was able to hold back the tears.

Whispering softly,"I have some news"

"Okkayyy... What do you have to tell me"

As I sat there on the phone with a long distraught pause,

She kept saying " hello hello are you there",

"Yes" hysterically

"I am pregnant"

She laughed because of course she thought I was kidding.

In defense mode, I yelled " NO I'M SERIOUSLY PREGNANT!"

And she paused on the phone "I'm sorry" in her apologetic voice

She began to explain to me how she understood how I felt because she hit this same milestone in her life before. The whole time she was talking, it was going on one ear and out the other because I personally didn't want to hear anyone else's story because I was in a dilemma myself. So I rushed her off the phone quickly because she wasn't helping my situation.

I laid stretched out on the bed with the pregnancy test lying diagonal from body, and I feel into a daze as if this was a dream, but my phone began to ring continuously over and over again... It was my mother calling, and I refused to answer.

I knew deep down that I needed to call my boyfriend, Mark, and tell him the depressing news. I began to rebuild courage again to make that call, my fingers slowly and barely touching the keypad to the dial the number, after each number I pressed I felt a teardrop run down my face unto the phone. So after about five minutes I pressed the talk button and he answered excitedly "Hey bae what you doing",

Instantaneously began crying and sniffling, and

He hollered "What is wrong? Is everything okay?"

I was crying so hard that I couldn't even catch my breath to say anything.

"Do I need to call your mom"

I hollered with a screeching halt "NO NO NO" ,

"You need to tell me now what is going on"

"Hold on", *as I put him on hold I took a picture of both pregnancy test and sent him the picture* "Check your messages",

Aggregately, "Why do I need to check my messages",

With a very rude attitude "Just check the message like I said"

"Is this a picture of what I think it is?"

Softly yes, "I'm PREGNANT" crying and yelling hysterically on the phone "My life is over, I'm another statistic, I have failed myself and my parents"...

"Just wait, calm down. First off we need to make sure that you are really pregnant, so you need to go the doctor office when you make it back to Mississippi".

"What the hell you mean, do you not believe me".

As I was talking, he was trying to over talk me and tell me to stop and calm down because I was blowing everything out of proportion.

This nigga decides to make a joke and say I told you I was gone put one in you. Oh boy, why did he say that it was like the ecstasy has rolled out of me, I jumped from 0 to 100 on him, and I went off calling him everything but his name and child of God. All kind of devilish thoughts were going through my head. So since he wanted to joke, I decided to take him there

"Well how much do you have because at this point in life I can't afford to stop my success for a child"

He got so enraged with anger you could hear the fierceness in his voice "I would never get rid of my child, and you are selfish to even say such a thing"

In the back of my mind, yes earlier when I first saw the results abortion did come across my mind, but I began to think about how I criticized and talked down upon those who did that, so my pride wouldn't allow me to take the human life away from an unwise decision I made.

As we were on the phone, he said I needed to calm down and he would do whatever it takes to make sure our child and I have the necessities of life. He and I were already taking care of one child he conceived before we entered into a relationship. Before he hung up the phone, I made him promise that he wouldn't announce to anyone the pregnancy because my emotions were making me think irrational. So as we hung up, he told me that he loved the unborn child and me dearly and everything was going to be okay in due timing.

After hanging up, I began crying again and slid my body from the bed to my behind sitting on the floor with my knees tucked under my stomach and I rocked myself back and forth back and forth. In swift seconds, I remember my bishop stating in his sermon, "Tears don't move God, but prayer and faith grab God's attention." As much as I wanted to continue to cry, I began praying and shouting to God in despair "Why me?" After all I was the churchgoing girl, I went to church faithfully, matter of fact I was there for Sunday service and Bible study, children church teacher, paid my tithes, and gave sacrificial offerings. But no instead, I was one of the few that fell into the realm of unplanned pregnancy. Filled with agony, I began to pray and ask God to remove me from this situation, let this not be so. But as I was praying I heard God saying you were chosen for this assignment, and if I put you in it, I'm God enough to bring you through it. As I heard those words, I began reflecting, *Weeping only endure by night, but joy comes in the morning.* I began reading my Bible on my cell phone and praying until I fell asleep, which gave me a calmness and easiness about myself.

My alarm clock on my phone was ringing louder and louder the longer I stayed in the bed and woke up with an excruciating headache. I rolled over almost falling out the bed, and the first thing sight was the pregnancy test with those two distinguishing blue lines. But I refused to start my day off in disappointment, so I prayed to God that He give me peace that surpasses all understanding. As I was getting dressed, I had to open my mouth and keep reminding myself I am God's child and everything was going to be all right. My phone began to ring, and it was my mom, and I suddenly went into a state of shock. I had yet to tell her anything. So I let the phone ring over and over again until the last ring and I picked up the phone acting normal as if nothing had ever happened. As my mom and I were talking on the phone, she asked

"Why didn't you call me back last night,"

"I fell asleep"

"How are you feeling"

I became paranoid because I felt she knew something was wrong, so I hurried and rushed her off the phone with a lame excuse.

As I was driving in the car to work, I turned to the gospel radio station in the car to ease my mind, but as I was getting to work, I began feeling knots in my stomach. I walked in the office pretending to be happy when deep down inside I was hurting with pain and shame. All during the day I couldn't focus on any assignment because my mind would replay to the devastating news of the previous night.

Around 2:00 that day, I couldn't take it any longer, and I ran to the back office to tell my friend at work what had happened last night. So Bee and I were joking and laughing as usual having a good time, and I looked at her in eyes and told her straight up that I was pregnant, and she looked and kind of laughed and off. I told her no seriously I am, and that I didn't know what to do or think. She asked how did Mark react and I told her he was fine with everything, and she told me she was excited for me and that everything was going to be great. At that moment, her positivity made me feel much better.

Revealing Pregnancy to Parents

After I left work that evening, my normal routine would be for me to call my mom and dad, but I couldn't convince myself to do so because I knew I needed to tell them I was pregnant. I know you are probably thinking, Girl, you a grown, educated twenty-three-year-old woman with a darn good job, why are you afraid? Well, unlike others, I'd tried to be perfect in every way possible. I was the type of person that didn't mind learning from other people's mistakes so I wouldn't have to endure the consequences. Everybody knew me as the innocent, smart, churchgoing woman who wouldn't dare do anything wrong.

I had the perfect plan to tell my parents I was pregnant without actually telling them... So this was my plan .. When I got back to Mississippi to hurry to move out my parents home, and buy an apartment, then send a letter in the mail expressing my pregnancy and how I felt because I was so afraid to tell them face to face. Woah!

My parents weren't intimidating or strict, they just put the fear of God in me, and I was more disappointed in myself because I felt like I'd failed them.

So, any who, I made it back to my hotel, and I knew good and well that my plan wasn't going to work. I sat in the car and pondered on what to say. What to do. How to react. I told myself you are stressing way too much because I can become very dramatic quickly.

I started practicing in my car how I was going to tell my mom over the phone, "Ma, if I tell you something, you can't get mad. I'm sorry but I'm pregnant," and so forth.

Finally, I built up the courage to call my mom, and as soon as she answered, I just spat, "I'm pregnant."

What?

I immediately began boo-hooing, and she said Megan why are you crying, you are a grown and successful woman and you are more than qualified to become a mom. I screamed mom my life is over with me, and I didn't want to enter parenthood at such an early age. She promised me that should would walk this journey with me, and God had full control. She reminded me that I was a young lady of virtue and I could stand the test of life. As we were on the phone, I begged and pleaded with her not to tell my daddy, and I would tell him once I knew for sure I was pregnant.

When I made it back to Vicksburg, I picked up my mom so we could head straight to the clinic to let the doctor see if I was really pregnant. My anxiety rose intensely as I open the clinic doors because this was such a surreal moment. When I signed into the doctor's office, I was immediately called to the back. The nurses at the clinic were some of the sweetest people you could ever meet.

The nurse saw the anxiety on my face, and she told me to just relax that everything was going to be A-OK. She took me to go the back room so they could draw blood and they could get a urine sample from me. After I finished the testing, my mom and I sat in the doctor's office, as I laid my head in my lap, I heard my mom snickering over the corner. I slowly picked my head up because I was wiping the tears from my eyes and I didn't want her to see me crying. She stopped laughing and she asked me was I crying and I told her no! I responded with what are you laughing at, and her response was life, and I said whatever nonchalantly.

The door began slowly screeching open and the nurse came in, and said with much joy and excitement "THE RESULTS ARE YOU'RE PREGNANT".

And I had a look of disbelief and slight blackout moment.

The nurse asked me was I okay.

I was so stunned I was unable to respond, it was like my mouth was moving, but no words came out.

My mom came beside me and hugged me and wiped away my tears.

The nurse said on file we see you were on birth control, so we are going to immediately send you to see an OBGYN because at the moment you are at high risk due to the birth control.

Not only was I nervous and afraid of the fact of being pregnant, but now I'm high-risk pregnancy so that put my unborn child and me at a potentially high risk.

They immediately sent me to the hospital so the doctors could run tests.

After I got the news, I called my boyfriend to confirm that I was pregnant, and surprisingly that gave him a sense of relief, but I didn't dwell on that because I had bigger news to tell him. So I went through the scenario of telling him that the doctor said the baby and I were at high risk due to the effects of the birth control, as I was explaining what was going on I could hear his voice becoming tense, shaky, and scared but he didn't want to show too much emotion because he was still at work.

I told him don't worry that everything was going to be okay and that God was covering the child and me, but in actuality I was really afraid and scared because I wasn't sure where my journey was going to end, but I had to step up and become strong for him.

In the car ride with my mom going to the hospital, I could feel my heart racing and pounding a thousand miles an hour, my forehead was glistening in sweat, my fingers and toes had a stingy tinkering feeling. My mom was talking to me, but my ears were numb as if I was hearing what she was saying but my brain was capturing the words so I couldn't understand. My whole body felt unbalanced.

My asked me was I feeling all right, and I slowly nodded my head up and down yes. The ride to the hospital felt like it took days because I was so anxious.

As I walked through the hospital doors, before I could enter the OB GYN part of the hospital, it seemed as though every time I turned my head I seen a big belly poking out as if they could have the baby any day. I entered the OBGYN office and signed in, and I felt very nervous and intimidated because I was ashamed of my condition. I honestly felt like I was another statistic.

The lady greeted me with much pleasure and a joyous attitude, and I gave her a phony smirk because I was overwhelmed I honestly forgot how to even smile.

The desk clerk said Megan we have been waiting on you and we are sending you to the sonographer immediately,

I politely said thank you.

So we sat in the waiting room for about ten minutes, and as I held my head down the entire time because I was afraid to look up because I just knew everyone was looking at me.

As we waited, I prayed that the sonogram would show that I wasn't pregnant and my life could go back to normal.

The door swung open heavily with a loud thumping sound, and the nurse called Megan Sullivan.

My mom grabbed my purse and we got up and walked to the sonogram room.

The technician had the most energetic attitude, and she asked me was I nervous.

I told her yeah somewhat.

My mom rubbed me on back and told me everything was going to be okay.

I undressed myself, and as I lay on the table, my body began trembling uncontrollably.

The technician asked me was I all right.

I told her I couldn't stop myself, and she responded saying that it was my nerves. I felt a slight tear roll down my face because I was really afraid. As she rubbed the cold gel across my belly, my body began to tense, all my muscles and joints became stiff. She took the tool, and rubbed it around my belly, and without any timing the little embryo was lying inside my belly, and she said with exclamation "There is the baby," from there I became emotional and I was smiling and crying because I was happy but yet disappointed in myself.

My mom had a smirk on her face, and she was excited about her first grandbaby. She told me that the baby was perfectly healthy.

So as the tech measured the size of the baby and my sac, and she told me I was approximately three months pregnant, and oh boy the look on face was like what in the hell is going on.

The tech saw the shock on my face and began telling me that I would be a great mother, and the road of motherhood was challenging, but I would experience some of the happiest moments in my life through my child.

In my head, all I could think of was that I had no choice but to have this baby.

She printed me out pictures of the baby, and she told me good luck as we were leaving out of the office.

As we were walking back to the front office to schedule an appointment with the OBGYN, I stared alarmingly at the pictures and thought that I was so unworthy to bring a precious child in the world knowing that I was unmarried.

My mom and I got in the car, and she said so when are you going to tell your dad.

I rolled my eyes to the back of my head and told her with a slick attitude that I was going to tell him soon. Telling my dad was the last thing I wanted to let alone tell but to even think about.

My boyfriend called me to tell me that he was coming down from his hometown right after he left work to come spend the night with me. The level of depression I was feeling went into total excitement because to see him would ease some of my pain, and this would allow us to come up with a plan in raising our child.

My mom and I finally made it home, and she asked was I hungry and I told her my stomach couldn't even handle the smell of food. When I made it home, surprisingly my aunt from Georgia was home visiting, because my Aunt Rose had just passed away from breast cancer. So she and my dad were sitting at the table talking and laughing, I tried to rapidly speak to her and my dad and run to my room. But oh noo I couldn't avoid them that quickly.

This particular day I had on some bright lime green linen pants and an everyday fitted white V-neck tee shirt, so the shirt was hugging my stomach a bit, so I had a slight pug overlapping my pants, but no one would ever guess that I was pregnant. You must realize at five four and weighing 120 lbs at the most, any weight gain would be noticeable.

My aunt hugged and kissed me, and jokingly said you have gained a little butt back there since last time I saw you, and she snickered. I laughed with her and brushed the comment off. My daddy poked me in my stomach, and I immediately began sweating and cringing and I told him, in my sweet innocent voice da stop, and he said you getting a bit chubby you better slow down eating those Debbie cakes and laughed.

Woahhh... I walked to my room so quickly and splattered on the bed with relief because that was a close call, and for a second I just knew my mom had told my dad without my permission. All I could think was, *Thank you, Lord!*

I called my boyfriend and asked where he was and said that he was almost in town, and was like okay babe see you when you get here, and before I could hang up he said you didn't tell your dad did you, and screamed with disgust ARE YOU CRAZY? NO!

And he replied saying I was just asking

and my response was uh huh. I knew this wasn't the time to tell my dad because he would wring a rope around my boyfriend's neck. We all know how fathers feel about their girls.

I laid in the bed playing on my phone, and I heard the doorbell ring, and I jumped out the bed, and opened the door excitedly for my handsome chocolate boyfriend because I hadn't seen him in days.

He spoke to everyone, and my mom gave him jokingly side eye, and he put his head down and laughed.

So before he and I could even have a conversation, my dad yelled and told him to come to the back room. He looked at me frantically and mouthed to me silently if I had told him, and I said with an attitude NO, then he asks did my mom tell him and I said not that of know of.

Raising up slowly from the couch, he looked at me and took a death breath and walked to the back. So I waited a couple of seconds before I walked to the back room because I was anxious about wanting to know why my dad needed him and not me.

My boyfriend played the normal with dad and they were joking around playing like normal, they always cracked up on short jokes amongst one another because God didn't bless either them with height hilariously. To see them laughing and joking eased my mind tremendously. My dad had purchased a new TV so he asked Mark to help him place it on the TV stand.

I walked from around the corner because I didn't want them to know I was eavesdropping, but I had to make sure the scene was clear. I went back to my room to get dressed for our date night.

As I was going through my closet, I was trying to find anything not to hug on my stomach because I was so insecure, but nobody noticed my stomach area but me. At times, I can be very dramatic as you may see. I tried on every freaking dress I had it was either too tight on my stomach, or too tight on my hips, or just didn't look right on me.

At that very moment, I sat in the middle of the floor and just began crying and all the thoughts of pregnancy, disappointment, sadness, and bitterness were running through my mind, and I felt like it was no way out.

Mark was screaming, "Megan, I'm hungry, hurry up before the line is too long."

I yelled back, "I don't want to go!"

Boom!

My door slammed opened and hit the wall, and he saw me on the floor crying and he responded saying "What the hell is going on"

the more I tried to respond the tears were flowing more and more. I cried so much it was enough for Noah's ark. I told him don't none of my clothes fit and I want a new life.

He looked at me and exclaimed with disgust REALLY, and he went through my closet and pulled out some jeans and nice loose fitting shirt and heels to put on. He grabbed me by hand and pulled me up from the floor, and hugged me tightly, and he slightly pushed me back from him and looked me in my face and said everything is going to be okay, and we gon' make it.

Eventually, I got out of my self-pity dried and got up off the floor.

He told me to hurry and dry my tears wash my face and so my parents would question what was going on.

I opened the bathroom door, got a washcloth, and ran the water to get the towel wet, as I picked up my head and looked in the mirror I just stared at my house and said pull it together not only for myself but for my unborn child. As I washed my face, a small tear fell down my face and I began to say repeatedly, "The joy of the Lord of my strength.", each time I said the scripture I began feeling a joy rise up in the inside of me.

I went back to room put on my clothes, jewelry, and makeup and brushed all the self-pity off and decided that I was going to have a good time. Right after I put on my clothes, I modeled back and forth, left to right in my long door mirror, and I took a deep breath and said to myself, "If you gon' be pregnant you might as well be fine and pregnant." Hmph, your girl confidence level went from 0 to 1000.

Click, clack, click, clack! I walked into the living room in my heels and my boyfriend look and me and smiled and snickered.

I side eyed him, nose flared wide and asked him what so darn funny."

"You just crazy, but I love you, babe."

I turned my head swinging my hair and said whatever and to grab my bags so we could go.

Getting our stuff together, my mom comes out the kitchen and makes the smart remark, don't make no babies.

, and he looked back and laughed and underneath his breath he gone say you a little too late for that.

and I glanced back at the both of them in disgust and said really. They are just cracking up laughing.

and personally I didn't find anything hilariously funny. Remember, it was only about thirty minutes earlier I was all out on the floor crying.

My mom went tell me stop being so sensitive, I might as well accept it and live on because being upset isn't going to rectify the situation.

Before we left, my mom sat us down and told us that she was disappointed because she knew that we would be responsible and great parents to this child.

Meantime, my mind was racing a thousand miles an hour, while she was talking... Just talking about raising a child scared me because I felt like I was not good enough. Starting to feel agitated, I started groaning because my stomach was growling and they were talking wayyyyy too much.

Mark gone tell my mama well let me get up and take your daughter to eat before she turns in the Hulk, and we all laughed and he and I went on our way.

* * *

We went to eat dinner and as we entered inside the door, all I saw were pregnant women, but the difference between them and I was that they were married. The waitress graciously guided us to our table, so as we waited I pulled my phone out and started scrolling through all the social media apps. Every couple of seconds I would pick my head up and look at Mark, but he was playing with his phone as well.

This one particular time, I looked up and he was staring so hard you could see the startling glare in his eyes. Self-consciously, I asked him politely could he stop staring, and he shook his head no.

Once again I looked down at my phone, and I glanced up and he was still staring. I began staring back at him, and I told him to stop playing, so he laughed and said smartly I can stare all I want too.

Rolling my eyes to the top of my head, I didn't even give him the privilege of a response.

As the food arrived, he gently began to have a conversation about the baby. The conversation started with I knew you were pregnant, and I was like how did you know if I didn't know, and he said your demeanor and attitude told it all. Disagreeing with his response, I told him I never changed.

* * *

Backing up in time, December of the previous year right after Christmas, his family and I were sitting on the couch laughing, talking, and having a great time. Mark's cousin was expecting a child, and she was just finding out.

and out of nowhere Mark exclaimed with joy, "Everybody, I have an announcement, and I would like to tell you that Megan is pregnant too."

and before I knew I yelled with a rude and mean attitude to him and everybody and I said, HE A LIE!

Everybody laughed, but I didn't find that funny at all.

In my past, I must admit, I was judgmental to those who barred children before marriage, and I vowed to myself to never become a statistic, and I would marry my Prince Charming and then we have kids, because I never wanted to be in the situation where I had to co-parent because I felt the child would lack in some areas of life, but God always has a way of humbling us.

As we were talking, he made a pivotal statement saying that we would need to find a central place to live together or either he would need to see if he could either find a new job in Vicksburg, or the possibility of his job allowing him to transfer to the store in Vicksburg.

In my mind I wasn't capturing this image he was trying to portray. In the middle of him talking, I stopped him and said ummm I don't particularly agree with that idea, and got very defensive and said why. I told him, I didn't think it was a very wise idea for us to move in together before marriage, and that was a moral that I was standing firmly on.

You could see the anger and disgust on his face, and he said that doesn't make any sense to me at all, we already have a baby on the way so what's the damn big deal.

I told him it is very much a problem because I never want to play house with a man, and you become so comfortable getting wifey privileges until the fact you feel as though you don't have to marry me because you are already receiving the benefits.

By this time, the energy was tense in the atmosphere.

He went say well how am I going to see and raise my child every day if we are not living together.

, and my response was you can stay some nights or weekend stays, or you could drive back and forth but making permanent living arrangements was a No Go. I was becoming very agitated during this conversation, so I quickly ended the conversation saying we would compromise on a plan and I changed the subject because I didn't want to argue out in a public.

When we finished eating, the original plan was to go to the movies, but my stomach started cramping as if I were on my cycle, and I began feeling lightheaded.

Mark said let's skip the movies and go to the hotel so you can get some rest, which I needed rest because I was out of town that whole week and I was consistently driving.

We were in the car driving, and I began discussing with Mark the importance of our relationship, and when I was telling him I didn't want to build a home together before marriage, I wasn't trying to pressure him at all, those were just one of my morals I had in my life, and yes I didn't want to have a child before marriage, but I did the action it took to have this child so now it's my , and before I could anything else, he said our responsibility to take care of this child.

I explained to him that I truly loved him and I only want the best for us.

He reached over the seat grabbed my leg tight and rubbed my stomach and said I love y'all too and I got us till the end.

Feeling so loved, my cheeks rosy, and I had the biggest kool aid smile you could possibly imagine.

When we made it to the hotel I was so tired, I crashed on the bed, as Mark was carrying the bags. That night he and I just talked and enjoyed one another.

The following morning Mark took me back home, and he left my home to spend the rest of the weekend with his daughter.

When I walked in the house, my mom came to room and asked so when are you going to tell your dad your pregnant.

I told her I am just give me a chance, I'm going to tell him today. As nervous, as I was you must imagine being a daddy's girl and you have to go tell him your pregnant, what a heavy burden that was on me, and then at the same time my aunt, which was his favorite aunt had passed away. So I wasn't sure if this was the appropriate time to let him know.

I built up the courage to finally tell him. It was a Saturday morning, and he was in his room trying out and playing with his new TV and folding clothes, and I said dad do you have a second to talk

he said sure I always have time for daddy's girl.

I was thinking in my head, I'm not sure if this the news you want to hear. I told him, I know you are going to be disappointed in me, and tears began rolling down my face.

he wasn't looking at me he just continued to fold clothes, he said what's up tell me.

And as I was saying that I was pregnant, I began crying.

He said what you crying for,

I said because I have failed in life and that I wasn't ready to be a mother, and I felt like I wasn't stable enough. Before he could say anything I told him, I looking for an apartment now for my child and I because it's time for me to step out on my own again like I was in Alabama.

He said hold up wait, baby you are grown woman, and I have no reason to be upset I knew something was abnormal with you anyway. He said one thing about parents we know our children. He said and furthermore you don't ever have to move out; he stated my favorite aunt just passed away and you think I'm willing to give up my child just because she is pregnant life is too short, and that child is blessing to us.

I was so shocked at his response because I was expecting a whole different aspect like for him to be mad and disappointed in me because I was the type of person that excelled in everything I touched. God had such a miraculous amount of favor on my life, me becoming pregnant was the first circumstance in life that I had encountered in which I felt like I was tail and not the head.

So after I told my dad, he gave me a hug, and he said now I'm not but I don't want to see that nigga for a couple of days.

I laughed and we went on about our day.

After revealing to my parents that I was pregnant, I felt like it was time to share the news with my bishop. I went up to him after Bible study one Tuesday morning, and I told him that I was expecting a child.

, and he said already knew it,

and I asked him had my parents told him

, and he said know I could see the change within you.

At that moment, I realized that my bishop was a true watchman over my soul unlike others I had encountered, he genuinely paid attention to his members.

I told him that I was ashamed of the predicament that I was in because not only was I pregnant, but I was pregnant without being married, and then I was still staying in my parents home, even though I had the money to move out and live on my on, but it was the principle of it all.

And he told me God uses every situation in our life to make us better but not to make us bitter.

Hearing that from him, I felt a sense of relief, because I knew he was only speaking what God was telling him say, and at that point that was what I needed to hear.

After telling my pastor, I told my aunt and cousins, and they were really excited because we hadn't had a baby on my mother's side of the family since my little brother, and he was eleven years old. So everybody was ready for a new baby.

Mark's parents were excited, but I wouldn't expect anything less from them knowing that they wanted us to be together, but this only pushed the issue of us becoming married. My desires were for Mark and I to get married before the thought of a child came in the picture, but everything happened so unexpectedly to the point I knew we were in the correct mental state to become married.

I was very ashamed of being pregnant because I perceived as the all-American perfect girl living in a perfect world, where everything was successful in everything I touched and I never failed in life. And *Boom!* right in my face I have slipped up in become pregnant before doing the proper actions such as marriage.

Thank God I wasn't showing in my pregnancy at all in my first trimester, because it wasn't hard for me to hide from the world that I was pregnant. I felt as though people would look down on me, and this would give people the opportunity to finally say, hmph she thought she was perfect, but finally she has messed up.

I assumed that people would be judgmental just for the simple fact, I was very judgmental of young ladies who had babies that were young or unmarried, and I thought that was the most unethical thing they could have done. But now I'm in the shoes of those same young ladies that I criticized and put down, now people have the opportunity to condemn them. But at the same time I felt like I still had the upper hand because, hey, I was twenty-three years, had a decent job, and my boyfriend and I had the potential of becoming married and raising our child together. So at least I wasn't a single parent.

I tried to validate myself throughout my pregnancy so people wouldn't count me as a statistic, but at the end of the day I was no different from those young ladies whom I'd criticized. Suddenly, I realized that I shouldn't judge so harshly and easily because in due time you do reap what you sow whether it's good or bad, what goes around comes around. And when you are in the heat and fire it isn't a good feeling whatsoever.

For a long time, I didn't tell people who weren't either my close friend, relatives or a part of Mark's family I was pregnant because I was truly ashamed. I would rarely leave out the house during my first trimester, and that wasn't a big deal at because my job in Alabama offered me the opportunity to work from home in Mississippi, so I had hardly had any reason to leave the house.

Let's Make It Last Forever

Mark and I decided it was time for us to begin planning our future together for the sake of the kids, the child he had before he got with me plus our unborn child at the time. We were potentially talking about marriage, and how we needed to start thinking about either him relocating to my hometown or me relocating to his. Relocating to his hometown would be no problem because my job allowed me to work from home. For the sake of me becoming a first-time mom, I didn't want to be too far away from my mom, which if I was to move it would only be an hour and fifteen minutes away, but it was the principle of me not being able to drive five minutes down the street.

Every weekend Mark would come down, and we would have a date night where we would take each other out to dinner or to the movies. So this particular night we decided to go out to eat, and we began having a discussion regarding our financial state, and the money we would have to spend on the baby.

So I began telling him how I received my first hospital bill, and my insurance didn't cover about five hundred dollars of my expenses.

I made the comment, "Man, I can only imagine how much it's going to cost to add a dependent to my medical insurance."

He said, "Yep. But that comes with having a child."

I looked at him strangely and said, "You right, because you will be contributing money to those funds. It isn't fair that I should pay for that alone."

So he went into saying, "It's all about money with you."

I told him, "No, it's not. But the reality of this situation is that money is going to be greatly involved with the well-being of not only the child we have together but also your daughter. So why are you becoming so defensive?"

"I just feel like this child is going to be so much more expensive."

I said, "We are really taking it this far just because I asked about money regarding health insurance for our child? Are you serious? You can go out and buy Polo shirts and all these name-brand shoes, but you have the audacity to act out about some money for insurance."

"Well, I didn't have to go through this with my first child."

"Yeah, you didn't because her mom qualified for assistance, whereas I don't because I make too much money. If I knew it would blow up like this, I would've never said anything. And, furthermore, I don't need your money. I can raise my child by myself. I can't deal with all this unnecessary drama; I am already going through enough pressure just being pregnant."

"No, *you* blew this up, and *you* are trying to compare the children. I don't have time for this, and I'm not going to deal with it."

I just gave him this long death-stare, trying to figure out where in the heck is all this coming from, because nowhere did I compare our unborn child and his daughter. I was really pissed off. I told him, "Fuck all of it! You don't have to ever worry about me bringing up anything regarding money at all because you're acting really ignorant."

Mark had a funky attitude, saying some hurtful things to me as if I was putting too much on him by discussing our child.

As we were sitting there eating, I was pretty pissed off myself, but I tried to hold it all in since we were in public. I told him, "You need to get over yourself."

Right then, Mark just got up from the table and walked out the restaurant.

I looked on in disbelief because he had never acted like this not one time since him and I were together, and now he was acting like a straight-up punk.

I continued to eat. The meal was too costly to just walk off, and secondly, since I had the keys to the vehicle, I decided to make him sit outside for a long period time. So while I was at the table eating, I felt myself become angrier and angrier to the point where I could feel the tears building up in my eyes. But I refused to cry in public over some nonsense.

I got up from the table, and I began walking to my car. I didn't pick up my phone to call Mark to see where he was, nor did I look around to find him, because if he was childish enough to get up from the table like a little kid and walk off, I was sure enough he could catch a ride somehow to get his car. I didn't care.

Then I realized I had the keys to not only my car but his too. So I was like, Forget this nigga! At the end of the day, he would still have to come up to me like a grown man to get the keys to his vehicle.

So as I walking in the parking lot toward my car, I saw him running across the parking lot.

He hollered, "So you was gon' try and leave me here?"

I just ignored him.

"I know you hear me but just act like you don't."

I unlocked only my side of the car. I cranked the car and got in.

He was beating on the door, "So you not gon' let me in?"

I politely cracked my window just a little to throw his keys outside on the ground to him, and I told him, "Find you a ride. Since you have so many issues with me, I think it's best we not be in the same vicinity." I drove off.

As I made it about ten seconds away from him, I heard God tell me to turn around and go back and get him. So I turned around.

I rolled down my window and told him, "Get in the car."

He got in the car and slammed the door.

God is my witness—it took everything in me not to snap out. I just kept thinking if God told me to go back and get him, He is God enough to keep me from laying these unholy hands on Mark.

As I was driving, we were both very silent; you could feel the tension in the car. So, me being me, I tried to start up a conversation. I said you might as well get over yourself and let this disagreement go because we in this for the long run now, boy." I reached over and kind of pushed him.

He looked at me as if to say, "Who you talking to?"

I just laughed, because laughing kept me from saying something really disrespectful to him.

We finally made it back to my parents' house. My mom and dad had left out to run some errands. I asked him, "You staying here tonight?"

And he said, "I guess."

I went into my mama's room and called my homegirl up to tell her what had happened. So as I was telling her that he'd said that I was trying to down him and his daughter because I told him he needed to contribute to our child medical expenses and insurance,

Now while I was saying all this, Mark didn't know I could see his shadow from behind the door as he snooped on my conversation. But I proceeded to carry on talking to my best friend because I was only telling the truth, and I needed someone to talk to about the situation.

So when I got off the phone with her, I opened the door—Boom! Mark was standing right in front of it shaking his head.

He said, "Yeah, yeah, yeah. So that's how you feel, huh?"

I walked past him and said, "Everything you heard was exactly the same thing I told you, so you know that's how I feel."

"Well, that wasn't anybody's business for you to go out and tell."

"Well, that wasn't none of your place to just sit there and listen like a fool."

So he began popping off at the mouth, saying, "I don't have time for this. I couldn't stay around you any longer because you're a fake and not a genuine person, and you keep downing my daughter and me."

I looked him in his face and said seriously, "How am I downing y'all? First of all, you the one that's taking everything out of context. Second, you just mad because I brought the issues of our finances. And, third, if you just want a reason to be mad, just be mad."

He said, "I can't stay here with you. I'm going home."

I opened up the door for him. "You could leave because I don't have time for the stress and added drama. I know I didn't do anything."

Furthermore, I felt like there was more to this story. Yes, maybe he felt pressured with this being his second child out of wedlock, but I felt the pressure also. But I didn't allow my reactions to discredit and hurt him.

After about ten minutes, I called Mark. I wanted to apologize to him not for what I said but for the way I said it in the heat of the moment, but he didn't answer. I called about three more times, and he didn't answer. So I sent him a text message: I HOPE WE CAN WORK THROUGH THIS. CALL ME WHEN YOU GET A CHANCE

Now normally when Mark was upset, he would walk away from the situation and cool off and usually return, but after about twenty to twenty-five minutes, I didn't see his car return down the driveway. So this had me a bit puzzled.

I kept trying to call him, but I didn't get an answer. So I was like, *You know what? Forget this. It's not even worth it.*

I went to bed that night and woke up about two in the morning, and I still didn't see a missed call or text message from him. At this point, I was kind of worried because I wanted to make sure he'd made it home safely. I was hoping that I didn't make him angry to the point where he did something really stupid.

All kind of thoughts played in my head, from him being on the side of the road, to being in a wreck, or even going out to see another girl. I began having flashbacks of him cheating and lying to me.

I called him again, and the phone rang twice and went straight to voicemail as if the call had been rejected.

Around noon the following day, he decided to call me, and I answered.

I immediately asked him, "Why did you ignore my phone calls? And where were you that you couldn't answer the phone?"

"I was pissed off and didn't want to talk to you in anger."

"That's not a valid excuse. Every time we have a disagreement you can't run off and think that when you come back around everything is going to be normal. I'm not going to accept that type of attitude anymore."

"You know what? I don't feel like arguing again."

"I'm not arguing, but we do need to have a conversation concerning our issues."

He went on to tell me that what I'd said the previous night was out of character and it wasn't right, that he felt as though I was comparing the children.

"That's bullcrap! Why would I compare the two, when that wasn't even the topic of conversation. Our conversation was about money and bills. Whatever, Mark. Think what you want. You have your mind made up, and you gon' believe what you want. I'm done with it."

* * *

Weeks went by, and it seemed as though our relationship was going downhill. Our conversations on the phone were dry and short, and Mark didn't put in the effort to spend time with me. It got to the point that the only time I would see him was when it was time to go to a scheduled doctor's appointment.

I would get excuse after excuse as to why he couldn't come down to see me, and then he would make statements like, "Why you can't come to me?"

I told him, "There would be plenty of times when I would go out my way to drive to come see you, but our normal routine is for you to come down to see me on the weekend."

We would just have pointless arguments over simple things, and I began feeling stressed and overwhelmed.

One weekend I planned for us to go to his church and out to dinner afterwards just so we could potentially get our relationship back on the right track because I wanted a family for me but most importantly my child. The Saturday morning before, Mark and I talked on the phone maybe twice before noon for a total of about an hour, and he told me that he was going to his little cousin's football game that morning, so I told him coolly, and we hung up the phone.

Well, I kept calling and texting him throughout the day, but I wasn't getting a response. I kept calling and calling. Then around four o'clock I got a text from him saying that he was going over to see his daughter because she had gotten sick and he would call me back once he left.

After about two hours had passed, I hadn't heard from Mark via text or a phone call. So I picked up the phone to call him. It rang one time and went straight to voicemail. I knew something wasn't right because he would talk on the phone with me while he was seeing his daughter, or he would text me, but I wasn't getting a response at all.

His mom had called me earlier that day, and I'd missed her call. I decided to call her to see if he was home. She said, "I haven't seen or heard from Mark since about noon when he left the house. He had a bag packed with him, so I assumed he was coming to stay with you."

I was on the other line of the phone like, *What is really going on?* but I remained calm on the line with her. She didn't know what was going on, so I played along with her.

I said, "Well, maybe he's on the road to my house. Let me give him a call." I hung up the phone.

Mark had no intentions of coming to see me, so I knew he was with some other chick. This was the last straw. I sent him a long text message: YOU OUT HERE IN THE STREETS PLAYING GAMES WITH ME, AND NOW YOU GOT ME PREGNANT AND YOU THINK I'M GOING TO SIT HERE AND TAKE THIS MESS, ONE THING ABOUT ME I'M NOT ABOUT TO PLAY ANYBODY'S FOOL, SO YOU CONTINUE TO DO YOU. I'M DONE FOR GOOD

As I was sitting in my bed, I began crying. Every time I put my all in him, all I got was a slap in the face. Now I was pregnant with his child and he was treating me like I was nothing.

I got on my knees and I prayed to God, "If the relationship is not destined for Mark and I, show me the signs, but grant me a spirit of calmness and peace. I am willing to accept the decision you have pre-destined for me, and I am able to withstand this storm because in Your word it says all things work together for good to those who love God and to those who are called according to His purpose."

I began to weep and weep, and I told myself you have to pull it together.

The next morning, I woke up and there was no missed call or text message from Mark. I wasn't going to pick up my phone to call or text him. I'd decided I wasn't going to put any effort into the relationship. So the plan was for us to go out to dinner, and no, that didn't happen whatsoever.

I received a text from him around five that evening: I APOLOGIZE FOR NOT ANSWERING YOUR CALLS OR TEXT YESTERDAY, BUT I AM GOING THROUGH A LOT OF THINGS IN MY MIND. I KNOW SOME THINGS ABOUT ME AREN'T RIGHT, AND I'M TRYING TO FIGURE MYSELF OUT. I REALLY NEED FOR YOU TO PRAY FOR ME AND BE HERE FOR ME DURING THIS TIME

I looked at the phone and for a moment, I felt sorry for him but then I quickly snapped out of it. *This is a bunch of bullcrap.*

I responded back to him about an hour later, telling him he isn't the only one going through something. Did he forget I was the one pregnant? I was going to be the one to receive the public shame from others because I was unmarried with a child. I told him I would pray for him, but his excuse was unacceptable to me. I told him, for one, he stood me up because we were supposed to go out on a date, and he still he never responded to me with a call or text, so at this point I didn't know what to think, or even if I could rely on him during the hard times.

He texted back: I APOLOGIZE AND I KNOW I AM WRONG. I JUST NEED YOU TO BE THERE FOR ME BECAUSE I AM STRUGGLING WITH SOME ISSUES

Later that night before I went to bed, I got on my knees once again and prayed to God that He reveal to me if Mark was the man He designed for me to be with, and if not He could take him out of my life immediately because I was tired of the continuous heartbreak. I asked God to shield me with His covering mercy and grace, to forgive me for all the mistakes I had made, and to cleanse me of all unrighteousness.

* * *

It was time for very my first doctor appointment since finding out I was pregnant, and I decided to go my mother's OB/GYN in Jackson because he had such a great reputation. Mark had to work a late shift that particular day, so I asked my mom to come along with me.

When we made it there, I was very nervous, but I was always fearful when it was time to go to the OB/GYN. Everyone at the doctor's office was sweet and so calm. They called me to the back and did the normal blood tests and urine exams before the doctor came in to examine me.

Dr. W came in and greeted me with a warm, vibrant voice as he introduced himself. He talked to me about becoming a first-time mom, and how exciting this point should be for me.

I explained to him how very tense and anxious I become when I take a vaginal examination, and he assured me that everything would be all right, that he would be as gentle as possible.

My mom looked at me and smirked. "Everything is going to be okay," she said.

Dr. W began the examination, but every time he would get close to being done, I would tense up. Unable to continue with the procedure, he explained to me how vital and important it was for him to check on me because he didn't want to run any risk of anything being wrong for the sake of the child.

After about three tries, he told me that he would have to reschedule me to come in because my anxiety level was way too high to try to continue. He left out the office and told me to wait on him because he got a call from his nurse. So as I waited in the office, I was so ashamed because my grown butt couldn't even go through a simple exam, and my mom explained to me that I would have to get over my fear because this was a requirement, especially with me carrying a child.

I said to myself, "God has not given me the spirit of fear, but of love, joy, and a sound mind." The more I said it. the more I believed it.

Instead of Dr. W coming back in the room, the nurse came down and asked if my mom and I would walk down to Dr. W's main office because he wanted to discuss some things with us. When we made it down to the office, he told us to sit down, and he handed me a bag with pregnancy magazines and self-help tools.

"As we were sitting down, he said, "We need to have a serious talk.""

I looked at him nervously because I wasn't sure what he was referring to.

He stated that it was important for him to do an examination on me because my urine examination wasn't clear.

I looked him in his eyes and asked, "What do you mean?"

"Are you having sex with one partner?" Dr. W asked.

I told him, "Yes."

"Were you having unprotected sex?"

"Of course," I said, "that's why I'm here in the first place."

He shook his head. He said, "Well, we found trichomoniasis in your urine."

I looked at him dumbfounded because I had no clue what that was, but I knew it was something bad because my mama started shaking her head.

He said, "It's an STD."

My heart dropped, my face turned pale, I couldn't feel my hands, and all I could see was black. Tears ran down my face, but I didn't have the strength to cry aloud.

As I cried in the office, Dr. W reached out a helping hand to both me and my mom, and all three of us prayed together. He said this is a curable disease, but we would need to wait till your second trimester to give you the medication.

I could barely move my body, and my stomach had a throbbing, nauseating feeling. I mean at this point there was no way Mark could lie, and say he wasn't cheating on me because the proof was in my face, this was the most daunting feeling a person could go through. I was afraid of how this disease could potentially affect my child, but Dr. W reassured me that there were no potential risks.

I was so embarrassed. I'd told my mom that I had a feeling that Mark was out there messing around, but I didn't want to find out this way, not in front of her.

When I made it home, I called Mark, and revealed to him the news that doctor shared with me, and, of course, he denied it all. He tried to flip on me, saying that I was stepping out on him when honestly at that point he was the only guy I was sleeping with. He was so offensive and aggressive, I could hear the guilt in his voice.

I was under so much stress and strain, I told him in a calm voice, "Well, whatever you think or say, we are at this point, and my doctor gave me a prescription to give to you to clear it up, so it's your choice whether you take it or not."

He hollered, "I ain't getting no prescription because I know I don't have anything. And, furthermore, how do I know you are not lying? You could be trying to set me up."

I said, "Really, this is something I would never lie about, but better yet when you come to my house tomorrow, I will give you the papers."

"Did you tell your parents?"

I lied and told him that they didn't know because if I told him they did he wouldn't want to come back around.

The next couple of days passed by and I just didn't feel a good vibe about Mark. I had a feeling he was hiding something from me, wasn't telling me how he truly felt. He was trying to avoid me.

One morning, I woke up with a heavy spirit on me, it was like I felt like I was carrying a heavy load on my back, and I prayed that God remove that burden from me. I just couldn't find my way that particular morning. It was as if everything that could possibly go wrong was going wrong, and I knew that wasn't of God.

In my spirit, I kept feeling the need to call Mark, even though in my flesh I didn't want to even hear his voice.

Around ten a.m. I called him because he didn't have to go to work till later that evening. I asked him, "Could we talk?"

He said, "Sure."

"We need to settle our issues," I told him, "because I don't like how this relationship is working out, and I can't continue to have this uneasy feeling."

"I understand."

"I have expressed myself numerous times, but now it's your time, and I know you told me you have a lot of things on your mind, so just tell me."

Long pause on the phone.

My heart began racing. I didn't know what he was about to tell me.

"I'm having commitment issues."

I said, "EXPLAIN!"

"I don't want to hurt you, but I'm seeing other women."

I remained calm. "Did you mean a woman or women?"

He paused for a while, and then he said, "I don't know why I'm telling you this because I want to be with you and don't want you to leave me."

I began crying on the phone.

"This is exactly why I didn't want to tell you."

Between sobs, I told him, "While I'm around here carrying your child, you are out here sleeping around on me. You have another girlfriend?"

"No, I don't have another girlfriend."

I asked, "So do these chicks even know I exist?"

He paused once again and quietly said, "Yes."

I am done! Because time after time you keep disrespecting me. I can only take so much.

He said, "Well, I want to work things out, and I'm willing to change."

"No, you're not. You think I'm some li'l rookie you can run around on?"

"Megan, I will always love you, and you will always remain number one in my life whether we are together or not."

After hearing that bullcrap, I just hung up the phone. I knew that was only God revealing to me to let him go because previously I dreamed I caught him sleeping around with another woman. I just sat in the bathroom and cried my eyes away, unable to stop the tears from flowing. And as I looked down at my belly, I felt distraught. I was bringing a child in a place of unhappiness and uneasiness, and it was all my fault because I should've paid attention to the warning signs.

So the first person I called was Mom, and I told her about the situation.

She said, "Baby, I'm on my way home," hearing the sadness and disappointment in my voice, and through my tears.

When she came home, she took me to my room and told me that God had already had a plan for my child and me, and that all things work together for my good. She told me not to put myself down, to pick my head up, and to stand on God's word because He said I am the tail and not the head, and I am above and not beneath, and I am more than a conqueror through Christ Jesus, who strengthens me.

But the tears in my eyes continued to flow.

She asked me, "Didn't you pray to God that he show you if Mark is for you? Now that it's revealed to you, you have to accept it and move on with your life. Don't ever settle when God has planned something better." She gave me a hug, but I knew she was very upset and just trying to hold it together for me.

I walked back to my room and saw a text message on my phone from Mark, and he was saying that he didn't want to hurt me, but I hurt him when I made the comment regarding my child not being on Medicaid and his daughter was, that I was trying to put them down.

In actuality, I was never trying to put them down. I was expressing to him that medical expenses were going to be significantly higher and that I would need his help with that.

I just looked at the phone because that was just an excuse he was using to try to cover up for his wrongdoings. I texted: YOU SHOULD'VE COME TO ME WHEN YOU HAD THE THOUGHT OF SEEING OTHER PEOPLE, AND YOU COULD'VE LET ME GO THEN INSTEAD OF DRAGGING ME THROUGH THE MUD, AND NOW I HAVE TO DEAL WITH THE PAIN WHEN I COULD HAVE AVOIDED THE WRECK BEFORE IT HAPPENED

He responded: I DON'T WANT TO BE WITH ANYBODY BUT YOU, AND FROM THIS DAY FORWARD I'M GOING TO DO WHATEVER IT TAKES TO GET BACK TO A BETTER PLACE

I never responded to his text message.

Throughout the day, he was continuously texting and calling me, and I never responded. I was so enraged, I didn't want to say the wrong thing during this critical time.

During this time my job had allowed me the opportunity to work from home, so as I was working from home, tears were steadily running down my face.

I decided to listen to T.D. Jakes' sermon on Youtube, a message titled "Nothing Just Happens." T.D. Jakes describes in the sermon how God allows us to go through obstacles and dispositions for a reason—to test our endurance and to see if we are able to withstand the tests of life because God has to test us before blessing us. That was the first message I heard on Youtube, God must've known in His infinite wisdom that's what I needed to hear.

As days went on, Mark would text me, but I just couldn't put my heart back in the right place to give him a decent conversation. I really felt shamed because now, not only was I pregnant but I was also a single mother. By this time, I was feeling like a walking statistic and outcast. I couldn't wrap my mind around how I got to this place in life. It was if I had done a 180, and there was no turning back.

Eventually, I gave Mark the opportunity to call and talk to me. Don't get me wrong, I truly missed him, but I knew deep down he wasn't what I needed. But after loving someone for so long, it was hard to let go. He and I had a soul tie, due to our having sexual intercourse, and I felt like a piece of him was within me, so it was hard just letting go completely. Each night I would cry in pity for myself. What people were going to think of me continuously played on my brain; I knew they would laugh at my pain.

Even though Mark and I weren't a couple any more, we kind of kept that understanding that we weren't going to get serious anymore because we were going to potentially try to work things out. I prayed to God that He would have mercy on us and restore our relationship.

So this particular day, it was time for us to find out if we were having a boy or girl. Our adrenaline was high, and we were anxious to know what we were expecting. This was the most we'd enjoyed each other's company since separating.

As we entered the room, the sonographer welcomed both us. She added, "Awww! Y'all are such a beautiful couple.

I just kind of shook my head and smirked. because If she only knew the hell we were going through.

As I lay across the table, I became very nervous. She rubbed the gel across my stomach, and within seconds she was able to tell us the gender of the baby.

She said, "Guess what? You guys are having a girl."

I laughed and smiled. I looked over to Mark, and he shook his head with a slick smirk.

Mark asked the sonographer, "Are you sure it's a girl? Could you take another look for me?"

"Most definitely." She rolled the device over my stomach, and she zoomed in and showed him that it was most definitely a girl.

I looked over and saw a small tear roll down his face, and he tried to wipe it away quickly.

The sonographer asked, "What's wrong?"

I told her, "He was expecting a boy; he already has a daughter."

She said, "Well, you have the determining the factor if it's a girl or boy—the male carries the dominant gene."

"Man, I need to apologize to all the women I've hurt because now I have two girls in this world."

I looked at him in disgust. "You right, starting with the first apology for me."

He just looked at me and shook his head, and he didn't open up to his mouth to apologize.

We rode back to my house after leaving the hospital.

As I got out the car, I told him, "Good-bye."

He said, "That's it from you?"

"Yes."

That evening, I had a "gender reveal" party, so I invited all my friends and family for drinks, food, cake, and just a good, ol'-fashioned time.

Mark's mother, Robin, came to the house and brought Mark's daughter as well. I was so excited to see the little girl because it had been about a month since I'd last seen her since Mark and I broke up.

While the party was going on, everybody kept asking, "Where is Mark?"

I told them, "He's at work," which he was, but only my mom, dad, Mark's parents, and my best friends knew that we weren't together anymore. I didn't make a public announcement to the world because I was too embarrassed and ashamed. I didn't want the label "baby mama." That was just so ghetto to me.

After everyone left, Mark's mom decided to stay a little longer, and she and I sat on the couch and talked. Mark's daughter asked if she could stay the night. Now normally I wouldn't have minded her staying at all because I loved Mya like she was my very own, but I was unsure if her dad would let her. So I didn't think it was appropriate for her to stay with me, under those conditions. So I told her she could stay another time ~~because~~ since I had to go to work the next morning.

Mark's mom asked me, "Is there a possibility of Mark and you getting back together?"

I responded, "Yes, I do miss your son, but I don't know that he is in the right state of mind to be fully committed to me."

She said, "I've been praying day and night that y'all get back together. He was so much better off with you than he is now."

"Well, I will call him tonight, and he and I will talk."

I sent Mark a text: SEEING MYA TODAY MADE ME REALIZE HOW MUCH I MISS MY FAMILY, AND I WANT US BACK TOGETHER

He replied after about thirty minutes: WE WILL WORK ON IT

WHY DO WE HAVE WORK ON IT? LET'S JUST DO IT

IT ISN'T JUST THAT EASY

So after Robin and Mya left my house, I reached out and gave Mark a call. It was around ten p.m., and I could tell from the background noise that he had to be in the car.

I asked him, "Where are you coming from?"

"I'm heading home."

I repeated my question. "Where are you coming from?"

"Man, why you asking all these questions?" he said with an attitude.

"Don't worry about it." Then I said to him, "Can you be truthful with me and answer one question?"

"Depending on what it is."

"You are acting really arrogant. I know I have made my share of mistakes, but I have let a lot of my pride go. But are you in a relationship with someone else? Is that the reason why you and I can't be together?"

He said with a really nasty attitude, "Megan, I'm gon' call you back."

"Just answer the question."

He hollered, "I will call you back once I make it home."

After I got off the phone, I wondered, *Why did I even set myself up for failure?* At that moment I knew it was time for me to move on and let go of the past.

Six Months Alone Rejected

After being rejected from Mark, and somewhat coming the realization that it was a possibility of us not being a relationship again took a toll on me. I never imagined being that girl who would have to endure her pregnancy alone without my child's father. I felt so cold and shallow, it was a though I was just waking up just to go to sleep again, I had no sense in my body I felt numb. As I looked around at all my friends, everyone was living there happy ever after, as I was hiding and pretending behind a veil as if my life was all right, but instead I was living in my own shadow of darkness. I would avoid people at all times, I would cringe when people would ask me about Mark, and I lie in their face as if everything was going fine. When I knew deep down that pain shattered deep down through my spine. I would shed tears and days and nights because of the journey that I had to embrace, while each day I prayed and prayed that God would shed His grace upon me, and I continuously prayed that God would make me stronger. Throughout the day, I would repeat, "Let the weak say that I'm strong," so that eventually those words would come into fluent. The only time I would smile is when I would get a random text and here and there from Mark checking on the baby and me, but that smile didn't last long because I would remember that my dream life was falling before my eyes, and my reality was waiting right there in front of me. My pain would turn into agony, I had begun to think of evil thoughts, I wanted a way to hurt Mark as much as he hurt me, but my heart wouldn't allow me to cause him any pain. His mom would call and I would cry out to her, and she would try to comfort me, and give me hope that one day Mark and I would get back together. And I kind of stood on her beliefs because even though I knew that wasn't what I needed, but that was what I wanted. I remember the time I went to Mark's church, and his pastor prayed over me, she told me that I was longing for a love that I wasn't receiving, and she prayed that I get that love I desired, and from there I got a sign that Mark wasn't supplying with the love that I deserved. His mother would call day and night to check on me, and she would tell me that God has made a strong woman, but on the inside I felt so weak and helpless. I knew that I needed to pull myself together because I didn't want my pain and burdens to have a negative effect on my child.

One day my godbrother was over at house, and he and I were talking, having a general conversation. I was telling him about how Mark and I weren't together, and how bad it took a toll on me. He was experiencing a bad breakup himself, but he told me to keep my head up because I was strong enough to endure the pain, and that I knew God so I needed to start acting on His Word. Even though all that was true, I told him its easier said than done. The Word was in, but I wasn't putting my faith to work. Instead I wanted to satisfy and please my flesh. He and I were on his Instagram page looking around at different people's pictures, and I ran across Mark pictures, so I decided to click on his page, and why did I do that. The first picture I saw was a picture of him and this chick laying across the hotel bed together dated on his birthday. I felt my heart drop to my feet, my hands began shaking, my eyes went blank I was in total shock. I couldn't believe what I had seen. Mark and I didn't follow one another on social media, so I wasn't able to see these things on my profile. My god brother looked and I and said, Megan, I'm so sorry, I didn't know I followed him nor did I know this was on his page because if I did I promised I would have told you. In a shaky voice, trying to hold back my tears I told him it's not your fault, and it was meant for me to see this because it was time for me to let go of the false hope of us one day getting back together. My mom, sister, and brother were in the living room as well, so I ran to my room, and I splattered on the bed on my stomach and began crying tremendously with tears. I had never been heartbroken before, to just assume that he was with somebody was bad enough but to actually see it was horrific. I was so hurt because he lied and told me he wasn't in a relationship with anyone and he truly loved me, and we would work on getting back together but yet and still my eyes seen different. Not only was he with somebody else, but he put the picture on Instagram, allowing everybody who knew him to see that he'd moved on. So the picture I tried to portray to everyone as if everything was all right was a lie and it was evident by the pictures he had posted. I was more embarrassed than hurt because I knew that people would look at me as if I were stupid, trying to be with someone who obviously had eyes for someone else. This act from Mark proved to me that he was feeding me all lies and he didn't love me nor respect me even with the point of me carrying his child, it was if I was a non factor. At this point, I was in a lost state of mind. I didn't know what to do. Should I confront him, or should I just let the Lord fight this battle? But my flesh kicked in, and before I knew I sent him text stating that him moving on without telling me and leaving on the blindside was very disrespectful and that I was hurt by it but I told him to believe me I will make it through this but it's sad of man who can make a child but yet still can't even have the decency to work it out with the mom, you were with me during the good times, but now that I'm down I'm in this alone.

After I texted him, I sent his mom a message telling her I no longer wanted any dealings with her because she knew everything that was going on and yet and still she was feeding me lies also, I felt that she should've been honest with me because it was no way possible if your son is living with you and his a new girlfriend that you don't know, she wasn't being genuine at all.

He responded in a defensive mode telling me I was taking everything the wrong and things weren't as what they looked and I told him to save the lies it is what it is and no longer could take part in the conversation, he ended saying that wasn't his girlfriend and it was nothing like that.

His mother calls me and tells me she had no clue he was with someone else, and out of respect I didn't say anything.

but okay but I began pulling back from her anyway because I felt as though she was lying to me. I was so hurt, I was as I was in a black pit it couldn't find my way up. The was the first time my dad saw me hurt and crying in this way and it hurt him, so he reached out to Mark and told him that he needed to make up his mind if he wanted to be with me or not, and if he didn't that was fine but don't continue to play games because now he has two daughters that are going to be living in this world, and he knew that he would never want his daughters treated the way he is treating me.

So mark responded angrily and arrogantly and told him you don't know everything that's going on and he would like for him to stop texting his phone. At that point Mark was being very rude and disrespectful no one went out attacking him, my dad was just telling him the truth.

My parents were fed up with the drama and lies, and like typical parents they were on the defense about him because they were tired of seeing my crying and hurt, and there was no way they could fix my problem. Over time it seemed as though I would cry about any little thing from seeing couples together walking in the mall with their children would make me depressed, looking on social media at people in love and having so much fun would me sick and cry, and to look on my life as a single mom I felt like I was at the bottom of the totem pole. So one particular day, Mark's new girlfriend decided to write on my best friend's Facebook page and say hi because they had previously had a class together, but my best friend didn't know this was the girl I was referring to as Mark's girlfriend. Of course the girl did this intentionally to be messy, but hey the spirit of the enemy never fights fair, he attacks where it hurt the most. So I went to look at the girl's Facebook profile, and the first thing I saw was pictures of her and Mark. Then there were pictures of him along with her kids, and she was writing statuses like he was there for her children, and he was a provider for them and how she was glad God placed a man like him in her life for her and her kids. That was an ultimate stab in the back for me, now yes if I wasn't up looking I would've had never seen these things, but at the same time I felt as though it was meant for me to see this to learn the type of person I was dealing with. I was so upset and enraged with angry because during this time Mark gave me every excuse in the book why he couldn't attend a doctor's appointment, or if I would ask him to go out and purchase necessities for the baby he would give me an excuse, but yet he could go out and take care of another child that wasn't his own. I came to the realization that it was just time to let go of all hope of Mark even being the man I needed just for support during my pregnancy.

At my doctor's appointments, I would look around and see couples of all races, supporting one another, and there me alone with my head sunk in my shoulders because of my own shame. I would think day and night, *Did I do something wrong?* or if there was anything I could have possibly changed the situation, but I had to remember that this was predestined for me, and if God didn't think I was strong enough to go through it and become a conqueror, He wouldn't have allowed it to happen.

Refining Process

Over time, I had to face the fact that I would now have to embrace my journey alone during my pregnancy and accept the role as a single parent. At this point, I knew Mark wasn't going to be there for me, but I was unsure if he was going to be the father I desired for my daughter. During this time I wasn't crying as much because I had to face reality that life just isn't as if we planned it out to be, we are sometimes thrown a curveball but it's up to us to either stand the curve and endure the ride or to try to dodge every obstacle that comes our way, but some obstacles are required to exceed to the next dimension in life. At times, I would get to my low points and become saddened and depressed, but one thing I knew my Bishop was only one call away. I remember calling him, and on this day I was having a really hard time just trying to get my mind right and focused, so when I called him he was so full of joy while me on the other end of the phone trying to hold back my tears, and I was telling him how life wasn't fair and how this journey is the most difficult thing I have encountered, and I didn't know how in was going to make it through. I knew my faith in God was unwavering and I didn't want to allow this journey to turn me into a state of bitterness. My pastor told me that with every success in life there is a failure, he said every successful person you know has encountered a failure or failures to get to their purpose. He told me that this situation is not designed to make me bitter but to make better, he stated that this was a process in which God was weeding out what I didn't need in my life and to humble me so he began to bless me. He said remember God always tests you before He blesses you. He told me now you are already person that loves hard and gives your all, and that's why you're in this state, but like in Hebrews 12:2 "And be not conformed to this world: but be ye transformed by the renewing of your mind, that you may prove what is good and acceptable and perfect in the will of God. He told you are strong enough to make it through because He wouldn't have allowed it if He didn't think you could handle it. He said now you need to put on your big-girl clothes, and stop crying because my feelings are going to be a reflection of the child and we both didn't want a sad and depressed child.

After speaking with my Bishop, I felt a shift in my spirit, and I refused to no longer let my mind go back into a state of depression. Why stress and worry about something for one that I couldn't not change, and for two I knew Mark wasn't losing any sleep over me so why was I even bogging myself down. Each day I would wake up around five in the morning to read my Bible, and I would pray before I read that God would place in my spirit what chapter and verse to read to enlighten my dead. After reading I would speak daily affirmations numerous times through the day:

"I'm the head and not the tail, I'm above and not beneath,

I can do all through Christ who strengthens me

I'm not conformed of this world, but I'm transformed by the renewing of my mind

All things work together for good to them that love God, to them who are the called according to *His* purpose.

I'm blessed in the city, I'm blessed in the field, I'm blessed going in, I'm blessed coming out

God has not given me the spirit of fear, but of love, joy, and a sound mind,

I walk by FAITH and not by SIGHT

Cleanse me of all unrighteousness, and draw me closer unto You,

Surround me with those who are for me, and not those who are intended to hurt,

Bless thine enemies, as You bless me

I would continuously speak the Word of God over my life to keep a positive and uplifting attitude throughout the day, when I would feel myself getting down, I would immediately repeat to myself, "The joy of the Lord is my strength, and I bind up the spirit of heaviness off my life." As long as I kept speaking the Word the more I would become stronger and mightier. I would rarely ever look at TV because it was so much negativity and it seemed as though every time I would turn it on the tv would be something to remind of my past, and I wouldn't allow my thoughts to go back. I would watch and listen to my Bishop's sermons, T.D. Jakes, Joel Osteen, and Joyce Meyers. I needed that encouragement throughout the day to stay uplifted, and I needed that continuous confirmation that God had me in the palm of His hands and I wasn't in this battle alone. For the battle was not against flesh and blood, but it was a spiritual fight, and I could fight that through prayer and supplication. I came to the realization that it wasn't Mark as a person acting this way, it was a spirit within him, so I began to go into deep prayer for him, asking God to shine His light over Mark's life, and give him the strength to endure this fight. Even though I went in prayer for Mark, I stayed my distance from him because I knew I wasn't mature enough to come in contact with him.

As I was going through the refining process, I had to pull away from not only Mark but his family as well, because when his mom would call she would always somehow bring his name up and I didn't need the constant reminder. Yes, I had forgiven them, but I didn't forget the pain he'd caused, so I didn't allow myself to become vulnerable again. It got to the point where I had a time limit for how long I would stay on the phone with his mom. It was intended to be ugly toward her, but I had to protect myself and my feelings. They didn't know the days and hours it took me to get to this accepting process, so I had to look out for myself. As time went on Mark would text me, but it got to the point where he would send rude messages, so I just stopped replying all together. So one day he sent me an email: YOU MUST HAVE GOTTEN YOUR NUMBER CHANGED BECAUSE YOU DON'T ANSWER MY CALLS NOR RESPOND TO MY TEXT MESSAGES. I told him no I didn't get my number changed but until he learned to respect me, I wouldn't entertain a conversation with him. So he became angry I didn't hear from him for weeks, which was totally fine with me because I was working on bettering myself, and I had to learn how to have a forgiving heart. because How can I not forgive a person here on Earth when God is a forgiving God? It was a long process of forgiving Mark, but I knew that was the right thing to do, so I ordered the book "" by Joyce Meyers, and she was teaching the keys to forgiveness, and one point that stood out to me was she stated so many people miss out on their blessings for the lack of forgiveness, and I knew at that point I had to let go and give it to GOD because I wasn't going to allow an unforgiveness keep me back from getting what God had in store for me.

I attended church every Sunday morning service, and every Tuesday for Bible study, and I would continuously get fed the Word of God. Now that I was single and my main focus wasn't on pleasing a man, I was able to encounter and establish a true relationship with God. Sometimes you don't realize how much you put into a person, and you're so into making them happy, you begin to lose yourself, and I was a lost cause trying to find my way back. So one particular day, my Bishop called me up to the altar from prayer, and he told me that Megan, God told me to tell you that you are not going through this for yourself but you are going through this for others, and he said for don't become weary in well doing: for in due season we shall reap, if we faint not. He told me to keep the faith, and God said it was done and all was well that I wouldn't have to suffer through the pain anymore, and God has given me beauty for ashes. He said Megan it is done and it is so, God has heard your cries and tears, but you just keep the faith you will see His unveiling hand. My mom was behind me and I got her arms and shed tears of joy and happiness because God knew I was withstanding the storm at such a vulnerable time.

About two weeks later, my Bishop invited another pastor/prophet to come to our church and preach, and the man pointed me out and told me to come up front for prayer. Around that time I was in the last trimester of my pregnancy, so I didn't have much longer to go before the arrival of my baby, so I waddled out my chair to the front of the church. He looked me in my eyes, and said oh ye faithful woman of God; God has seen strength, endurance, and faithfulness, there have been people who laughed and been amused by your struggle and shame, and who have done you wrong, but God will get the last laugh, don't you worry what people have said or done because God is going to bless you for your faithfulness. He said eyes nor ears have seen the place where God is going to excel you, he said this battle isn't for you, but it is for you to share with those who will encounter this same breaking point of life you have come to. He said and your child will be blessed, she will bring you and those she encounter great joy, he said that child is Blessed from the crown of the head to the soul of her feet. All I could do was give God the glory because good continued to confirm to me that he had me and that al that I was going through was just taking me to the next step in life.

One night I went to the emergency room because I was bleeding it was about four weeks before it was time for me to have Madison, so my mom rushed me to the hospital because we wanted to make sure that everything was okay.

So out of respect, I called Mark several times attempting to let him know what was going on but he didn't answer, so I called his mom and told her, and she asked did she need to come down to the hospital and I told her no, I had my mom, and I would be all right. So when I made it to the hospital the nurse on duty gave me an examination and the baby was perfectly fine, but I had burst a small blood vessel, which was normal during pregnancy, but she told me that I needed to get plenty of rest, and stay off my feet as much as possible. I made it back home around ten that night; I got in the bed and began reading my Bible till I fell asleep.

During my last trimester of my pregnancy, I would wake up numerous times throughout the night. So I woke up to a text message from Mark stating this "Gn I really don't wanna see anything happen to either one of y'all. I know I've been the reason for most of the stress. And I apologize for everything. But I've been working in done change a lot. I'm gon' be the best for our child. But we have to do better both of us and what we say toward each other", and I responded back "Yep, I accept it and I pray you do get better", and he responded saying "Some things I should've put my pride to side about, but you are an amazing woman", and I reassured him I know my worth. Even though he sent me those messages, I still wouldn't allow myself to fully believe what he had said because I had heard the apologies on numerous occasions. But hey I was willing to forgive, so I didn't get out of character.

Grace Is Sufficient

Time was winding down, and it was getting closer for me to have my baby girl. I decided on the name Madison Grace, because the name of Madison was a derivation from the name Matthew, which meant a gift from God, and the name Grace came along because it was by God's grace I was able to survive the storm.

The morning of October 21, 2014, I felt some slight cramping and I was a little woozy, but I just endured the pain and thought I could sleep it off as I normally did. Now that night that my doctor had scheduled me to come in at midnight to induce my labor, but boy things just didn't go as planned.

Around three that afternoon my cramps began to worsen, but that they were endurable, but I called my mom and I told her I think we need to go the hospital, so came home in a rush got my bags, and we were headed to the hospital.

When I got to the hospital the doctor put some pain medicine in my IV, and we she checked me, and she looked at me and said you came in at the very last minute because you are 7 cm dilated, and I looked at her and said what, and she looked at me in shock because she couldn't believe that I had endured the pain for that length of time. So she hurried and called the anesthesiologist, and he came in and gave me an epidural.

Before I left the house I had called Mark and as mom and I told them that I was headed to the hospital. So maybe about thirty minutes when I made it to the room, his mom came in and stayed there until she had to go to work, and I was so drowsy I barely even recognized her.

About an hour after I was settled in the room Mark and his daughter came in the room, and it was like drop dead silence when he walked through—my mom, aunt, and my mom's best friend just stared at him as if he was a zombie. So I kind of broke the ice and spoke to him, and he said hey to everyone and they spoke back.

I began getting very hot and irritated. Mark brought me over some ice and tried to rub my hand at that particular moment I didn't want anyone to touch me because I felt pain even when somebody looked in my face. I snatched back from him and he looked at me as if he was shocked but at that moment I didn't care what anybody thought. I was just ready to get that baby from inside of me out.

Finally, the time had come for me to push! Adrenaline was running high, my legs began to quiver, and I was in the state of excitement and nervousness. The nurse came in and asked who I wanted to stay in the room with me and I chose my aunt and my mom, and Mark looked at me in despair. I didn't think it was appropriate for him to stay with me, for one he had his daughter with him and she didn't need to see that, and for two him and I hadn't really socialized, and I needed support. So he picked his daughter up and walked outside in the foyer to wait until I had the baby.

After looking and caressing my precious daughter, they allowed him to come in the room and hold her before they took her to the nursery. Mark held Madison in fear and hold her in his hands

"This child is a spitting image of me"

Jokingly "I beg to differ"

"You just don't want to admit it"

"She just came out the wound how can you even tell who she resembles"

That night he left because he had to take his daughter back home, and my mom stayed the night with me. My child brought me so much joy and peace, words can't explain. All the time during those months, I finally gained the most valuable gift life could offer, and it was all worth it in the end. My child was full of joy and life, a ball of happiness.

That next morning, Mark called to check on the baby and me, and he asked me to send him pictures so I did. I stayed in the hospital over a course of two days, and Mark didn't come back to visit the baby. But I didn't act on it all. The office manager came to my room to get some information concerning the baby.

"What are you naming your precious newborn?"

"Aww, Thanks! Madison Grace Sullivan"

"Are you going to add the father to the certificate"

"At this moment, I don't think that would be a wise decision to do, so no mam",

Looking at me strangely, "Are you sure?"

Adominatly, "Yes, I'm sure, I'm making a very sound decision"

If Mark cared enough to his name on the birth certificate he would've made his way back to the hospital so I wasn't going to grow the hassle of calling him and begging him to come down to do something that he knew he needed to do, and honestly I didn't want his name on the certificate anyway.

When I made it home his mom and cousin popped up my house unannounced, which was very unmannerly, to come see the baby; I mean, thank God, my mom didn't have a problem with that because I was staying in her house. Mark didn't call or ask if he could come along with them to see his newborn child. But I had made up in my mind before I had Madison that it was a ninety percent chance that I would be a single mom so it bothered me a little, but not as much as it would've in the past.

My friend called me up and tells me the reason why Mark wasn't trying to see Madison was because he had left and went out of town the following day I had the baby with his new girlfriend. Now that pissed me off; how ignorant and selfish could you be to leave your newborn child and go out and hit the streets, but it didn't surprise me at all because I didn't know what kind of person Mark was, but I sure knew it wasn't the Mark I had dated because his child always came first, or maybe it was the mentality that I had that a child always comes before your significant other. By that point, I was just fed up with him, and I wanted to cut all ties, but I kept saying this is not for me this is for my child so I'm going to allow him the opportunity to establish a bond with his daughter.

Mark would call to talk to Madison on facetime, and each and every time I would have the camera looking directly at Madison and I wouldn't be anywhere in sight. He would always make little comments as if he wanted to see me and try to make flirtatious remarks, but I wasn't going for it at all. My attraction for him had disappeared. Yes, I had love for him, but I wasn't in love with him, and trust me, it's a major difference.

One Step Forward, Two Steps Backward

After having Madison and bringing home was an adjusting period for us. From the late nights to the early mornings, from feeding every three hours, to changing diapers so much I couldn't even keep a record. Well, during that time, I was becoming stressed and overwhelmed because I was continuously on the go and there was never time just for me. I loved my child dearly, but trust, a lot of work goes unknown with being a single parent. Mark would call and text me saying he was going to buy milk and diapers, and that he was going to be there for our child, and yes, at first I believed him, but as days and weeks went by, I didn't see any diapers or milk nor did I see him.

Mark would call about three times out the week to check on the baby. On this particular day, Mark called me, and I let the phone ring until I assumed it was the last right before it went to the voicemail.

"Hey, how are you"

"I'm straight," I said very dry

"I really apologize how everything went down, and I know I was the cause for a lot of stress"

"Honestly, you don't have to apologize anymore, It is what it is" *while twirling my finger around gesturing whatever.* "The past is the past and I have moved on"

"Megan let's try to make this co-parenting thing work out, we are in this together, and you and I are going to provide the best possible future for our child"

"Sure, I will" *sarcastically, I would allow my hopes to rise, Mark had only been proving me wrong the entire pregnancy*

"Seriously, you mean *we*",

As we were talking, he made the mention about us becoming a family,

"Ummm don't think that will happen at all"

He paused on the phone as if he was surprised I rejected him

"You are Madison's father, and I'm her mother, and that's the way it will remain because all of us becoming one just isn't going to work for me at all"

My goals and desires in life that I'm trying to accomplish only involve God, my child, and me. He changed the subject on the phone, and began talking about he was going to get a tattoo with Madison name and his first daughter's name, and my thoughts *were that is the dumbest way to try to impress me, so irrelevant, try spending that money on some darn diapers.*

I was so nonchalant because Mark thought he was doing all these great things, but he didn't know that I knew that the whole time I was pregnant he was out in Atlanta with some chick, so nothing that came out his mouth could validate him nor his actions, but I kept that to myself. I felt as though I would broach that issue at the proper time.

So one day he asked to come by house to see the baby, and my mom and dad were just irritated with him because throughout my pregnancy he'd left me alone, and then when I had the baby he was just there for the birth, and we didn't see him anymore. Mark was just in a bad place with everyone, and I totally understood where my parents were coming from because they were looking out for my well-being, and they didn't want to see fall back in that pit. I told Mark that in order for him to come to my parents' house, where I was staying, he needed to apologize to my dad for disrespecting him over the text message.

I told him that was out of character and out of line, so therefore the least you can do is apologize before walking in this man's house, he said I don't see the point of me apologizing he the one that came to me, I didn't come to him and if we wouldn't have said anything we wouldn't be in this predicament and further one that wasn't none of his business nor his place. In my calm voice, I said okay then Mark, I just pray that your daughters never encounter a man of your character, because what you done unto others do come back on you. I said I pray each and every day that I break all generational curses off my child because I don't want her to have to suffer for our actions.

By this time, he had become mad and started popping off at the mouth, making comments like "ain't like the baby got my last name no way, and if I don't see my child I won't do nothing for her, and you ain't got nothing, and you'll regret doing me like this because at the end of the day Madison is going to hate you for this". Politely stated," You know what, Mark? I can't even talk to you because me having nothing has never been the case, and you talking out of rage, and my daughter will never hate me, if I ever told her how you have abandoned her, you would get more of the dislike rather than I, but you continue to pop off at the mouth. And as far as Madison, I promise not one day will she go without anything with or without you, so goodbye. I hung up the phone in his face.

After I got off the phone with him I began crying because he had hurt my feelings, even though the things he said about me were untrue, but it was so unfair how I had to take care of this child that I didn't make by myself. If anything even if he didn't want to do anything at least he owed me some type of responsibility toward our child, seeing I was there and did all that I could for his first daughter, and she wasn't even my own flesh and blood.

I learned quickly what you do for others you don't always get in return, and those whom you love the most are the ones who hurt you the most, and that's because you open your heart up to them so much that you become vulnerable. After shedding those tears, I told myself I would never allow him to get me that angry and upset because he does have rule over how I feel. I sent Mark a text message saying that if he couldn't talk to me out of respect that he doesn't need to call my phone at all and I meant that.

I knew that I was giving into my flesh, so I got on my knees and prayed, and as I was praying I could hear a voice saying, *"This is not working against you, but this is working for you. Just keep faith, and I will show you your way out, and your tomorrow is so much better than your today."* I began weeping and praising God because I knew that this crisis I was in was only to mold and shape me into the woman God purposely designed me to be. I had to continue to rely on the Word of God, and at this time, I couldn't allow myself to become vulnerable to the outside world.

Madison was about two months when she started daycare because I had to return back to work. She was in daycare for about two weeks before she got sick. My baby was having trouble breathing, she was coughing, and she had a severe runny nose. So I immediately took her to the doctor, and they informed me that she had a respiratory virus infection, so my next question was, "How did this come about?" The doctor stated this most likely came from daycare, where another child might've had the infection and passed it on to Madison, and she said we need to test Madison to make sure we don't need to keep her in the hospital. I began crying and getting upset because my baby was so young to be this sickly, and to get sick from other kids.

After going through multiple x-rays and breathing treatments, they allowed me to take Madison home, and they made us watch her under very good care. She was placed on a breathing treatment for the next ten days, so I called Mark and told him what was going on, and he asked did he need to come down, I told him that she goes to the doctor the following week and he could come if he liked, and he responded saying that he would definitely be there.

So the next week rolled around, and I didn't remind Mark of the doctor's appointment because if it was that important to him he didn't need reminding.

That morning, I texted him and asked: ARE YOU COMING DOWN FOR MADISON'S APPOINTMENT, I'M GOING TO TRY TO MAKE IT. To keep from getting pissed off, I didn't respond. So about five minutes later, I got a call from him, and I let the phone ring about three times before I answered, "What time is the appointment again" with an attitude

"I told you nine",

"yep okay I will be on my way"

"Don't feel like you obligated to come because she good, whether you're there or not, I understand you to have other priorities"

" I said I was coming,"

and I just hung up the phone because he acted as if it was an inconvenience for him to come when this was something for his child.

Madison and I made it to the hospital about eight thirty, and we waited in the waiting room for about fifteen minutes, and we seen no Mark, so I was just whatever. The nurse called us to the back, and still no sight of Mark. The doctor did the routine checkup on Madison, and after she was finished, she and I were talking. Just then I heard the door crack open, and it's Mark. So I looked at my phone and it was nine forty,

The doctor just stared at him, and asked who he was, and he told her. She looked back at me and said, "Megan you are doing an excellent job as a mother, and I will see you next time, and you have my number if you have any problems." She looked him up and down as if he wasn't supposed to be there and walked out.

He looked at me and asked me how was Madison doing and I said she good, and there was just an awkward silence, I refrained from saying much because I was pissed at the fact he came when we were done so he had no intentions on even being on time. He grabbed Madison and she was hollering and screaming because she was in pain due to her getting shots. He was attempting to proceed to calm her down rocking her side to side, "It's going to be okay daddy's baby", and the disgusted look I had towards him and shook my head and laughed silently because he didn't know what to do.

"So what are yall about to do?"

"I need new tires, so I'm headed to TD Tires"

"Oh, so who is going to watch Madison while your getting tires"

Turning my head and looking at him crazy, "Who else?, Me"

"Do you mind me following you, so I can watch her while you handle business"

Deep down I wanted to say NO, NOT ALL, I couldn't' stand this boy! "That's fine"… I mean it was going to help me out and this way he could spend a little more time with Madison.

When we made it to the tire place I got out the car and he got in my car grabbed Madison and walked back to his car, and I looked at him and told him to come inside with my baby, he wasn't going to keep her in the car, and he looked at me and took a deep breath but I didn't care one bit.

The technician who was working on my car was somewhat flirtatious, but that was just him he didn't mean anything by it, as Mark walked in behind me, the technician smirked. The tech called me to the back to talk to me about which tires I needed …

"So that's your boyfriend "

and I can quickly and frankly "no not at all", and he laughed.

By that time Mark and the baby were in the waiting room so when I walked in Mark gon' say, I see how you do, and I just looked and ignored him. I sat across the room from him, and he began making comments to the baby saying "Your mom doesn't love me anymore, your mama is mean but I still love her no matter what and your mama want give us an opportunity to have a family."

He was trying to make himself look pitiful, but Mark was a character so I just kept ignoring him. My car was finally finished about after an hour of sitting there during that dreadful time with Mark. He and I made it outside to the car and as I was putting Madison in her car seat, Mark rubbed his hand against my butt. I jerked around and pushed him and asked, "Have you lost your mind? You really need to step back".

Laughing arrogantly "So you don't miss thi-"

" NO, NOT AT ALL."

"You need to go ahead and leave, and furthermore don't you have a girlfriend to attend to"

"N'all I just have a friend",

"Whatever she is to you, you need to respect her and leave me alone."

As I was walking to get in on the driver's side, he opened my door, and smile, and I pulled him back from the door because I didn't want to be bothered. He had crossed the lines

"Not gon' give me a hug,"

"No, Have you lost your mind? You and I will never be on that level again."

I was trying to close the door, and he kept holding it open,

"Seriously come on because I need to leave."

So he finally closed the door, and leaned over in the car, and asked me did I need anything and I told him no, and he kept reaching and car, and I was leaning back. I told him to get back and he didn't so I put my car in reverse and began backing up and he gone say so you gonna drag me with the car, and I told him I asked you to move and you wouldn't, so I guess so. He finally moved from my car, and before I could get down the street good enough, my phone was ringing. It was him, and he gone say let me know when you get home and don't be speeding with my daughter in the car, and I said, "Mm-hmm," and hung up the phone. Mark began reaching out more at that point, and Madison was getting older so I was getting better with the idea of allowing her to go with him.

As Madison reached about four months, she was able to leave the house and go out with places. At this time, I gave Mark the opportunity to spend one on one time with Madison. Now, believe me, it was so hard to leave my child with him unattended because I had all types of thoughts run through my head. Like at one time Mark had threatened to take me to court, and take the baby away from me, which I knew wasn't going to happen because for one his name was on the birth certificate, he didn't have a valid reason to take the child from me, and thirdly he didn't want to pay the cost to hire a lawyer and pay court fees. That was a stupid idea anyway for the simple fact that I didn't even put him on child support.

Now the average single mother would have put him on child support the day she stepped out of the hospital door, but I had remorse on Mark because he had already had another child, and he was stretching his funds trying to take care of her and himself, so I didn't want to put that strain and stress on him.

Now most of y'all probably looking like why she feeling sorry for him with all the hell he put her through, but God blessed me with a great job with excellent pay, so I had the funds needed to fully take care of Madison's needs and wants without a struggle. I met up Mark, and he got out the car and smiled and said hey, and I looked at him and said hey and turned my head and began getting Madison bag together, so he came from around my side of the car over to Madison, and the grin he had on his face was large and vibrant as if he had seen his long-lost brother. So I grabbed the car seat and I was giving him directions on how to take care of Madison, how she ate, and how many times he had to change her, and he looked at me with a smirk saying you act like this my first time with baby, and I responded in a smart sassy manner saying well this the first time you have taken care of my child, so these are the directions you need to follow. Now I was already on edge about letting her go with you, so your best bet is to just to listen, and he said okay Megan whatever pleases you. So his daughter was in the car, and she acted if she wanted to speak but she was afraid so I spoke to her and I didn't treat her any different because what issues me and her father had no reflection on how I treated her.

After allowing Madison to visit her father, I assumed that when Madison would come back home with me he would either have bought her some things or at least offered me some money, but that didn't happen. I felt I shouldn't have to ask, that he should just do that automatically, but my pride wouldn't even allow me to ask him for anything because he knew she needed items. I just fell to my knees and continued to pray to God that my heart doesn't become hardened toward Mark, and He cleanse me of all unrighteousness. I asked that God mold Mark into the man he needs to be for his child and that He also help me with my flaws in life and guide me through parenting. And I left it in God's hand from there.

Restored by Grace

Through all the turmoil, pain, embarrassment, and ridicule, I made it out strong as a conqueror. Romans 8:38 states, "Nay, in all these things were are more than conquerors through him that loved us." This journey was not yet easy, and yet this was still the beginning of God's divine plans and promises. Throughout the journey I learned that obstacles are placed in your life to strengthen and humble you. As I began to mature, I realized that it wasn't Mark acting out, but it was more so a spirit within him and began praying against that spirit. Even though I had no intention of getting back in a relationship with him, but I continued to pray for and still to this day I pray that God bless him abundantly, that He allow our relationship as parents to grow in a manner that is favorable to our child, and I ask God to forgive me for holding on to any bitterness and unforgiveness toward him. As I prayed, I left the issues between him and I, and I allowed God to take over. In due season and due time, God will have a deliverance and restoration period for Mark and Madison.

During this season as a single mother, I continuously stayed prayed-up and grounded in God's Word because this is a time when we must pray in order to survive through life because we aren't fighting things of the norm.

Ephesians 6:12 (KJV): "For we wrestle not against flesh and blood, but against principalities, against powers, against the rulers of the darkness of this world, against spiritual wickedness in high places."

I began progressing exceptionally at my job, and my faith in God was at a whole new dimension. I have learned the things that I was praying about, God had already confirmed those things in the Bible, and I just needed to speak those things into existence and believe because what God had for me was for me, and no man can take that away.

At this point in my life, several guys tried to engage with me on a relational basis, but I knew they weren't of God, so I didn't waste their time nor mine. Just because I was single didn't mean I was ready to jump into a relationship. I promised myself that I was going to stay whole and faithful, and not give into my flesh, and not make a move unless it was ordained by God. Before entering into a new relationship, I pray that God prepares me as He prepares the man that awaits for me, as he should my daughter and I as Christ loved the church, a man of valor and a man that's favorable unto the Lord. Before engaging in another relationship, I want to be fresh and whole and able to give my all once again as before. I pray that God gives me a spirit of discernment to recognize those who are for me and those against me.

This season of my life helped me to mature and change in areas in my life that I didn't realize were in shambles. I found myself so involved in pleasing others, that while alone I didn't know myself, and was trying to define myself through my relationship with others. This time of loneliness was designed for just me and God and no one else. Every other person who tried to enter my life during this time was quickly removed because God said this was my season of weeding and growing, and there was only enough room for the two of us. I didn't realize the amount of hatred I had buried in my heart from my own insecurities, but God brought me into a season of deliverance. As I pondered on the name of my child, I chose Madison Grace, not knowing that I was prophetically naming my child. I was God's child, and all I needed was Grace to make it through the storm. Along this journey, yes, I'd made mistakes, but my mistakes taught me lifelong lessons to mend my broken heart. When I'd first found out I was pregnant, I was afraid and ashamed, but I quickly learned that God hadn't given us the spirit of fear, but of love, joy, and a sound mind.

I thought that I had wasted three years of my life in a relationship that ended in a dead end, but instead I learned that God can restore those wasted years, and use them in such a remarkable way that your eyes and ears couldn't imagine.

Joel 2:25–32: "And I will compensate you for the years That the swarming locust has eaten, the creeping locust, the stripping locust, and the gnawing locust— My great army which I sent among you. You will have plenty to eat and be satisfied And praise the name of the LORD your God Who has dealt wondrously with you, And My people shall never be put to shame."

As I look back on this journey, during our times of storms, we should follow the habits of an eagle, the sharpest and highest amongst all birds,

Eagles hang with eagles; they don't hang with those beneath them. When eagles find themselves in a storm, they don't run from the storm, but rather uses the storm's wind shifts to rising above it, and this capability allows them to rest during the storm. So while we are trying to fight our way out of the battle, if we let go and let God handle it, we can just ride the storm out, and God will bring us out. As believers, we accept the storms and challenges in life, and we use them for us in a positive manner. Eagles have strong vision, which allows them to stay focused on their plan and agenda, and it doesn't allow doubt and disbelief to get in the way of their success. Lastly, as an eagle begins to grow and become wiser, his feathers began to fade away, but as those are fading away he begins to grow new feathers, and we go through situations in our life where they are pulling off the bad habits and we are becoming renewed.

Isaiah 40:31 (NLT): "But those who trust in the Lord will find new strength. They will soar high on wings like eagles. They will run and now grow weary. They will walk and not faint."

I never for once thought that I would be the one chosen for this walk through life, but God chose me because He knew I had the tenacity to win this race, but His plan is way better than my plan because this phase of the journey has ended with me in so much joy and peace. I can truly say I love Megan because now I have had the opportunity to meet me. Never let your past talk you out of your future because your tomorrow is so much greater than your yesterday. All you need is a mustard seed of faith to trust and believe that, even though you don't see a way out, God has already made a way out. I love the way my Bishop says it, "While you trying to figure it out, God has already worked it out." As I end this journey, God has prepared a new place for me in life. As I end, remember God gives us new and refreshed grace each day.

www.ingramcontent.com/pod-product-compliance
Lightning Source LLC
Chambersburg PA
CBHW060947040426
42445CB00011B/1035